Reseller Assortment
Decision Criteria

Jerker Nilsson
Viggo Høst

Reseller Assortment Decision Criteria

AARHUS UNIVERSITY PRESS

Copyright by the authors, 1987
Typesetting by Werks Fotosats, Aarhus
Printed in Denmark by Special-Trykkeriet, Viborg
ISBN 87 7288 079 1

AARHUS UNIVERSITY PRESS
Aarhus University
DK-8000 Aarhus C
Denmark

Simultaneously published in hardback by
JAI PRESS INC. as supplement no. 3
of the "Research in Marketing" series.

CONTENTS

PREFACE

Reseller assortment issues are of great importance for many specific social groups as well as for societal development in general.

- For the manufacturer, the resellers constitute the road to the ultimate market. Hence, it is necessary that he knows the resellers' assortment decision making so that he can make sure that his products are distributed through and by the resellers.
- The composition of the assortment can be regarded as the key issue for the reseller. The assortment determines which market segments the company attracts and what competition it faces. Hence, it has decisive importance for the company's sales, costs and profits.
- How the assortments are arranged in the stores affects the consumer's possibilities of getting her needs and wants satisfied. This concerns the functional and emotional characteristics of the products as well as prices and various services in the stores.
- As seen from a macro perspective, the assortments are closely related to the entire societal development. The interrelated assortment changes at all levels of the distribution channels constitute a moving force in society's economic and material development. In a modern, Western society, the totality of products sold and consumed is the most important carrier of culture.

Despite this surmised significance of the composition of reseller assortments, theoretical understanding of the subject is fairly limited and unstructured. The literature on reseller assortment decision criteria may comprise many titles, but nevertheless, it consists mainly of descriptions of what criteria have been used in single reseller companies on certain occasions. What is lacking are explanations of how the resellers' criteria are related to the various situational factors. To get a deeper understanding of the subject matter, it is imperative that such relationship patterns are uncovered.

This book is an attempt to remedy this shortcoming of earlier research. On the basis of an empirical study of a large number of assortment decisions in a specific reseller enterprise, the authors identify various patterns of decision criteria. Further, these patterns are explained in relation to the various characteristics of the reseller enterprise (history, ownership, strategic positions, organizational setup, etc.) and to the characteristics of its business environment (supplier attributes, competition, consumer demand, etc.). The result is a comprehensive and integrated exposition of the contingencies of reseller assortment decision criteria.

In a conference paper a couple of years ago, the authors reported some preliminary findings from this research project, which deviate somewhat from those presented in this book. (Høst & Nilsson 1983.) These differences are due to the fact that some refinements in the coding of the data set have been made in the meantime.

The authors bear a joint responsibility for the book in its entirety. Nevertheless, Nilsson being specialized in marketing and Høst in statistics, it is evident that the work has been divided between them in a specific way. Nilsson is associate professor at the Copenhagen School of Economics and Business Administration and Høst is associate professor at the University of Aarhus.

The study is based on data material which Kooperativa Förbundet, Stockholm (The Swedish Union of Consumer Cooperatives) has made accessible. This is acknowledged with great gratitude. The authors wish to express their deep appreciation to some of their colleagues who have been particularly helpful in carrying out this project. Hans Stubbe Solgaard, of the Copenhagen School of Economics and Business Administration, and Jens Vestergaard, of the Aarhus School of Economics and Business Administration, offered valuable criticism and made suggestions which have contributed to greater clarity on many points. Aage Erhardtsen and Svend Hylleberg, both of the University of Aarhus, made constructive comments on an earlier version of the manuscript.

Thomas Einfeldt assisted with the EDP computations. Gitte Jønsson typed most af the manuscript. Some parts of it were typed by Kirsten Stentoft. We wish to extend our warm thanks to all of them.

Finally, the authors wish to express their gratitude to the institutions that have supported this project with financial aid: the University of Aarhus, the Copenhagen School of Economics and Business Administration, the Danish Social Science Research Council and the Research Foundation of the University of Aarhus.

Copenhagen and Aarhus, Denmark
December 1986

Jerker Nilsson and Viggo Høst

SUMMARY

This study concerns the choice criteria used by resellers in their decisions about assortment changes. A thorough survey of previous research within this field is presented. Based on this literature survey, an empirical analysis of the assortment decision criteria used by a specific reseller firm is conducted. The findings show that, depending on what type of decision it concerns, different sets of criteria are applied, and it is possible to give plausible explanations of these differences. The overall conclusion, from both the theoretical and the empirical part of the study, is that trying to determine the relative importance of the criteria in a generally valid way is an impossible task. Rather, in order to understand the influence of various criteria, one has to take into account a variety of situational variables, pertaining to the specific decision case.

A review of 34 previous studies on reseller assortment decision criteria shows a remarkable heterogeneity as to which criteria are reported as significant. This heterogeneity can be explained by the fact that most often the studies present descriptions of criteria, found to be applied under widely varying circumstances. As to the importance of various criteria, the main common trait is that the prospects for sales and profits of a product seem to be the dominant criterion for the assortment decisions. Other criteria, often reported as important, are the supplier's introductory marketing campaign, the supplier's reputation and the price and the allowances of the product, but the significance of these criteria varies considerably.

Though it is not possible to deduce the relative importance of the various criteria from previous research, one can, however, establish categories of every conceivable criterion on the basis of these studies. Such an exhaustive list of criteria is suggested:

- Profitability and sales
  Overall profitability; Rate of turnover; Sales potential
- Economic conditions
  Supplier's price; Gross margin; Allowances and rebates; Support to cooperative marketing; Credit terms; Other economic conditions
- Assortment considerations
  Existence of distributor brands; Relations to other products
- Consumer evaluation
  Overall consumer value; Retail price; Product's physical characteristics; Product's psychological characteristics; Package
- Supplier marketing
  Introductory marketing campaign; Continual marketing

- Supplier characteristics
  Supplier   representative;   Reputation   and   reliability;   Salesforce
  organization; Services and functions; Other characteristics
- Competitive considerations
- Distributive factors
  Transportation adaptation; Store adaptation
- Salesman presentation

The empirical part of the study is based on the Swedish Union of Consumer Cooperatives. This is a large conglomerate with more than 2300 retail outlets of various kinds - hypermarkets, department stores, supermarkets, superettes, etc. Its market share in the food sector is 21 percent. It has also a very high degree of vertical integration. Hence, the organization owns a large number of production units, producing a rich variety of distributor brand products, and the headquarters has a significant influence on the assortments of both the regional warehouses and the retail outlets.

The study deals with the assortment building function at the central wholesale level, i. e., at the headquarters. Here, there is an assortment committee, which makes the formal and final decisions. In all other respects, the decision cases are, however, handled by buyers. When the buyers have completed their analyses, they fill in so-called product fact sheets, and as these are handed over to the committee, they serve as the committee's main decision basis. The product fact sheets contain a variety of information about the product under consideration (supplier name, package size and type, price, delivery time, supplier marketing plans, consumer panel test results, etc.) and also about all the products within the product group in question (supplier name, package size, price, sales volume, warehouse coverage, etc.).

The data sources for the study are product fact sheets which were presented to the assortment committee at three sessions, spread over one year. There are 54 product fact sheets with one product group per sheet and with a total of 506 products. Of these, 87 are new product offerings, while 419 are old products, i. e., already in the assortment.

In order to increase the chance of significant findings, the data set is split up into more homogeneous groups. Three variables turn out to be the best ones for this categorization: new products versus old products; distributor brands versus manufacturer brands; product groups without distributor brands versus product groups with distributor brand products. Considering that each group must be of a minimal size to make statistical computations meaningful, there are, however, only seven decision categories defined:

a. New manufacturer brand products
    78 product decisions - 38% accepted

b. All new products (manufacturer and distributor brands)
   87 product decisions - 45% accepted
c. Old manufacturer brand products in product groups without distributor brands
   261 product decisions - 90% retained
d. Old manufacturer brand products in product groups with distributor brands
   99 product decisions - 77% retained
e. Old manufacturer brand products (c + d)
   360 product decisions - 86% retained
f. Old distributor brand products
   59 product decisions - 88% retained
g. All old products (manufacturer and distributor brands, e + f)
   419 product decisions - 87% retained

On the basis of the information given on the product fact sheets, 14 decision criteria (explanatory variables) are isolated together with the decision outcome (response variable), i. e., retention or deletion of old products and acceptance or rejection of new products. The criteria are:

a. Sales trend of the product group
b. Size of the product group
c. Gradual change in the product group size
d. Existence of distributor brands in the product group
e. Price per unit of weight or volume
f. Package size
g. The product's degree of newness
h. The product's share of product group sales
i. Supplier identity as market leader
j. Whether the product is a distributor brand or not
k. Supplier introductory marketing campaign
l. Sales trend of the product
m. Number of regional warehouses carrying product
n. Size of store for which the product is recommended

It is readily understood that all these criteria are not applicable for both old and new products. Hence, for the old products, 12 criteria have potential value (criteria a, b, c, d, e, f, h, i, j, l, m, n), while 10 criteria can be used in new product decisions (a, b, c, d, e, f, g, i, j, k).

The statistical technique used is logistic regression analysis. The application of this technique results in a number of identified criteria for each of the decision categories.

a.   Acceptance/rejection of new manufacturer brand products
A new manufacturer brand product's chances of being accepted are greater

- if there are no distributor brands in the product group (criterion d),
- if its price is low (cr. e), and
- if the supplier conducts an introductory marketing campaign (cr. k).

The common denominator for these criteria is the profitability goal of the chain. As for price and marketing campaign, these are both indicators of future sales of the product, and hence, they are directly related to the profitability of the chain. The reason why the existence of distributor brands may hinder a new manufacturer brand is evident: as the distributor brands give higher per unit profit the chain wants to protect them from stiff competition from manufacturer brands.

b.   Acceptance/rejection of all new products
New products tend to be accepted

- if the price is low (cr. e), and
- if the supplier conducts an introductory marketing campaign (cr. k).

There is a large overlap between this decision category and the preceding one, so the rationale for these two criteria is the same as in the previous category. The existence of distributor brands does not show up as important here, which it was in the preceding case. When it comes to the acceptance of new distributor brands, it should rather be regarded as positive if there are already some distributor brands in the product group, so that they can support the sales of the new ones.

c.   Retention/deletion of old manufacturer brand products in product groups without distributor brands
An old manufacturer brand product in this decision category has a greater chance of remaining in the assortment

- if its supplier is not the market leader (cr. i),
- if it is carried by a large number of the chain's regional warehouses (cr. m), and
- if the assortment committee recommends it for large retail outlets only, rather than for both small and large stores (cr. n).

The first of these criteria can be understood only in the light of the history and policy of this specific chain. It has, throughout its history, learned that it must struggle for independence. So, it cannot come as a surprise that it is somewhat cautious about market leading suppliers.

If a product is carried by many warehouses, its sales are probably satisfactory, and it is considered as an important item, so it is natural that it is not dropped. The last criterion really refers to the character of the product. It says that when products have a specialty character, it is more difficult to change from one brand to another.

d.   Retention/deletion of old manufacturer brand products in product groups with distributor brands

These manufacturer brands are more likely to remain in the assortment

- if the product group is large in number (cr. b),
- if the size of the product group increases (cr. c),
- if the supplier is not the market leader (cr. i), and
- if the product has a positive sales trend (cr. l).

The first criterion is an expression of the product character, though of a different kind than in the preceding decision category. Here it means that in large product groups, the relations between several of the items are often so close (they have, in a way, a basic character), that it is difficult to make any changes. The second criterion shows up as important, because the data set in this decision category contains several so-called assortment reviews, meaning that a number of products are deleted simultaneously.

The explanation of the third criterion is the same as in the preceding decision category, i. e., the reseller tries to avoid becoming dependent on the strongest and most dominating suppliers. Finally, it is quite natural that products with bad sales trends are deleted.

e.   Retention/deletion of old manufacturer brand products

An old manufacturer brand is more likely to be retained

- if the product group is large in number (cr. b),
- if the size of the product group increases (cr. c),
- if there are no distributor brands in the product group in question (cr. d), and
- if the product has a positive sales trend (cr. l).

This decision category is an aggregate of the two preceding ones, hence the explanations for three of the four criteria are bound to be the same. The new criterion is the one concerning distributor brands in the product group, and the reason why this turned out to be important is found in the general differences between the two constituent categories. For the reseller, it is rational to be particularly attentive to distributor brands, so he is more prone to delete manufacturer brands which are competing with the distributor brands.

f.   Retention/deletion of old distributor brand products
The old distributor brands have a greater chance of staying in the assortment

- if their sales trends are positive (cr. l), and
- if they are carried by many regional warehouses (cr. m).

These two criteria are clearly related to the sales goal of the chain, thus also to its profitability goal. Old distributor brands are deleted when their market positions have been irrevokably weakened.

g.   Retention/deletion of all old products
Old products' chances of staying in the assortment are improved

- if the product group is large in number (cr. b),
- if the product group size increases (cr. c),
- if there are no distributor brands in the product group (cr. d),
- if the product has a positive sales trend (cr. l), and
- if the product is carried by many regional warehouses (cr. m).

This decision category is an aggregation of the two preceding ones, so it is natural that the identified criteria are a mixture of those presented above. As all these variables have already been discussed, there is no reason to elaborate further on them here.

Even this very short synopsis of the findings demonstrates that there are logical explanations behind all the criteria used in the various decision categories. Moreover, one can also see that there is a common, coherent pattern of the criteria in all the decision categories. The core of this is the reseller's profitability goal. The differences between the decision categories are due to the fact that each decision category has its own specific conditions for profitability. For example, if a decision concerns or affects the reseller's distributor brands, it is a pervading trait that the decision outcome will aim at supporting these distributor brand products. For the reseller, such a policy is only rational, due to the very different cost structure for distributor and manufacturer brands.

Another general conclusion is that the number and character of criteria seem to vary with the decision's degree of complexity and importance. In decision categories where the decisions are perceived as difficult and important, there tends to be a larger number of criteria and more elaborate ones. The decision makers not only look at the product's own characteristics, as they do in simple decisions (e.g., decision categories c and f), but they also undertake more complex analyses of the product group's attributes and the product's relations to other products (e.g., decision categories d, e and g).

1 PROBLEM

1.1 Introduction

The "assortment" dimension of retailing operations is clearly a matter which demands the attention of top management, for decisions in this area will "color" the entire character of the enterprise. However, once the general strategy is established for the organization, the tactical task of choosing specific products or brands usually falls to functionaries called "buyers". Buyers play a central role in retailing; unlike their counterparts in manufacturing concerns, their status within their "home" organizations is very high. Because buying is such a critical aspect of retailing, it is important to understand the evaluative processes and procedures that take place in vendor selection. (Stern & El-Ansary 1982, p. 55.)

The reseller product selections are, however, important not only for the resellers themselves, but equally for the manufacturers, as suppliers of the products, and for the consumers, as users of the products. Despite the general recognition of its great importance, the cumulative understanding of reseller assortment building is, however, fairly restricted. Hence, the aim of the study is to contribute to this field of knowledge. More specifically, it deals with the evaluative criteria used in the resellers' assortment composition decisions.

By assortment or, synonymously, product mix, is meant "the composite of products offered for sale by a firm or a business unit". (American Marketing Association 1960, p. 19.) All the products of an assortment have certain common characteristics, otherwise they would not belong to one and the same assortment. There must be a homogeneity of some kind and to some degree. For example, they might be produced from the same or related raw materials, be meant for similar uses, attract the same buyer categories, be purchased from the same supplier or require the same handling facilities.

All these are, however, only partial homogeneities, conditioned by the assortment possessor's quest for efficiency. (Alderson 1965, p. 33.) Hence, these and other common characteristics cannot be elements in a general definition of the concept of assortment; but they can only work as additional specifications, i.e., when defining various types of assortments. The only characteristic which the products have according to the general definition, is that they are all offered for sale by the same seller. In the selection of products for his assortment, the seller, then, may seek to obtain various types of partial homogeneities.

Hence, assortments are always to be found with sellers, and likewise, all sellers have an assortment. In other words, there is a direct correspondence between the concept of seller and the general concept of assortment. With additions to the assortment definition, however, the seller can also be regarded as having several assortments. A supermarket can, for example, be said to have one assortment of goods and another of services, or one of fresh goods and another of dry goods, or one of fruits and another of vegetables, or one of apples and another of oranges, etc.

It is, however, also possible to approach the concept of assortment from a more fundamental viewpoint, whereby a broader definition evolves. Seen in a broader perspective, an assortment could be defined as a set of products which an actor has for using in a specific type of activity. As activities are goal-directed, this definition is congruent with that of Alderson: "Assortments are collections which have been assembled by taking account of human expectations concerning future action." (Alderson 1965, p. 47.)

This broader definition deviates from the former to the extent that the actor could have other roles than a seller; hence, he could use the products for other purposes than selling them. The same distinction is made by Alderson, when he points out that the broad definition of assortments includes a narrower one of seller assortments, which, in effect, is identical with the concept chosen as the basis af the present study. "Intermediate assortments (trade stocks) have been collected to provide a choice of alternatives for (a) the consumer, (b) others in the trade." (Alderson 1965, p. 47.)

The extended definition of assortment can be used, for example, in the following situations:

- The manufacturer buys an assortment of raw material, which is intended to be used in the production of finished goods - procurement or purchasing assortment. (See Gümbel 1974, p. 1889, and 1976, p. 3564.)
- As the manufacturer produces, an assortment of finished goods builds up, to be used in storage activities for a certain period - storage assortment. (Gümbel 1976, p. 3564.)
- The producer then sells parts of his various storage assortments. The total amount of goods sold is a marketing or sales assortment. (Gümbel 1974, p. 1889 and 1976, p. 3564.)
- As the consumer is shopping, she selects an assortment of goods, pays for it and carries it home - procurement or purchasing assortment. (Wind 1977, p. 12.)
- In her home (refrigerator, freezer, cupboards, etc.) the consumer keeps an assortment of food items, which is used when cooking and eating - storage assortment. This corresponds to what Alderson calls an ultimate assortment: "Ultimate assortments (consumer inventories) have been collected by the consumer in the hope and expectation of being prepared to meet future contingencies (probable patterns of behavior)." (Alderson 1965, p. 47.)

Nevertheless, it is the first-mentioned, narrower assortment definition, which is valid here, as this study focuses on reseller assortment building - how resellers compose their assortments of goods offered for sale. The latter, broader definition is added to lend perspective.

This study comprises an analysis of a specific reseller. The organization is characterized by a high degree of integration, i. e., it conducts both retailing and wholesaling, and also manufacturing within a number of product groups. Only the wholesale business is examined here. The enterprise's wholesaling function is divided between a central level, which composes a nation-wide assortment, and a regional level, which, on the basis of this large central assortment, selects products for the regional assortments. The study concentrates on the central level, i. e., it treats the assortment composition within the various product groups which the central level offers to the chain's regional level and retail level.

Assortment building is regarded from the angle of the reseller. One could also analyse the assortment decisions as they appear in the eyes of suppliers, consumers, public authorities and other parties, but these perspectives are not included in the study. This approach is based on the conception that, when one is seeking insight about internal organizational matters, one should collect information from within the organization and also try to grasp these matters in the same manner as the organization does itself. In a way, the researcher should try to internalize the roles of the officers and the conditions for their decision making.

This does not, however, mean that the reseller's interest should guide the study. On the contrary, the study's character of independent and basic research should be stressed. It seeks to contribute, at a general and theoretical level, to the knowledge about assortment building within resellers, using the firm under study as a case. The study does not aim at producing any recommendations for immediate action by resellers, manufacturers, public authorities or other parties. Instead, we hope that there are lessons to be drawn at a more general level, not only for these types of parties, but also and especially for researchers and students interested in retailing and related fields.

When considering assortment building, the question of what factors determine the composition of the assortments arises. Among such factors, the assortment decision criteria of the seller have a prominent position, but there are evidently also many other factors behind these. This study focuses on assortment decision criteria. But it also strives to elucidate various background factors, in order to give explanations as to why certain criteria are used and are important. (See Section 1.5.)

Hence, we can formulate a preliminary and general statement of the aim of the study (paragraph (a)). Since subsequent sections will result in further qualifications (paragraphs (b) to (i)), the final formulation of the aim of the study cannot be presented until the end of this chapter.

(a) The study aims, through an empirical analysis, to contribute to the general knowledge about assortment decision criteria used in reseller organizations. The empirical work deals with the criteria applied at the central wholesale level of a strongly integrated grocery chain in its decisions regarding the composition of the assortment which is offered to the regional wholesale level and the retail level of the chain.

The book is arranged in the following way:

- Chapter 1 discusses the general, theoretical bases of the study. Aside from certain conceptual analyses, the chapter treats various matters of relevance for the object, the approach and the design of the study. The chapter can, therefore, be concluded with a specification of the final aim of the study.
- Chapter 2 presents further theoretical conditions, but of a more specific character. It comprises discussions of the previous research on reseller assortment decision criteria, including overall characterizations, attempts at systematization and a state-of-the-art review. Throughout the chapter, implications for the present study are discussed. This chapter is supplemented with an appendix, which systematically reviews 34 previous studies of reseller assortment decision criteria.
- Chapter 3 delineates the empirical basis of the study. It presents the reseller enterprise from different perspectives, the data source used and the variables of the study.
- Chapter 4 describes choices and designs of statistical methods and models.
- Chapter 5 reports the findings of the study, i.e., which criteria are used, under what circumstances, and why.

After the preliminary problem statement in this section (1.1), a discussion of the role of assortment decisions within the total marketing mix of the seller follows in Section 1.2. The problem analysis proceeds with a treatment of the character of reseller assortment decisions and buying decisions in Section 1.3, and the differences between assortment decisions of resellers, producers and public organizations in Section 1.4. The most central concept of this study is decision criteria, and these are, therefore, analyzed in Section 1.5. Finally, Section 1.6 reaches a more precise formulation of the object and the aim of the study by synthesizing the conclusions from the preceding sections, stated as paragraphs (a) to (i).

1.2 Assortment Decisions in the Marketing Mix

There are always numerous and close interrelations between all the decision parameters which a seller uses in his marketing effort - both cost relations and demand relations. A company's assortment affects its price policy, its advertising, its service measures, etc. Likewise, there are influences in the opposite direction, e.g., the price policy has implications for assortment changes. Hence, the entire marketing mix of the company can be regarded as a large and complex system. Likewise, the various classes of marketing decision variables, e.g., the four P's, cannot be considered as separate systems, as there are important interrelations between various product policy decisions, various pricing decisions, etc. (See Kotler 1984, p. 72-73: Product, Price, Place and Promotion policies.)

The fact that there are interrelations between the marketing decision variables of a company does not, however, mean that all variables are of equal value. Within a system, one can often identify a so-called leading subsystem. (Rehnman 1973, p. 35.) This is one part of the system, which has greater significance for the functioning and the development of the system than has the other parts. It may be that one of the marketing decision variables influences the others more than it is influenced by them, thus constituting the core of the marketing mix.

The assortment composition can often be considered as such a leading subsystem within the company's marketing mix system. (Gümbel 1974, p. 1884.) The company's assortment has profound effects on the structural characteristics of the company. It determines in what industry the company is, what segments it attracts and what competition it faces. Making comprehensive assortment changes is generally a time-consuming, costly and risky project. The assortment plays a dominant role for the image which the company has among its customers. It is basically the products constituting the assortment which decide the customers' interest in the company. All of this argues that assortment decisions are the leading subsystem of the marketing mix, thus implicitly justifying the fact that this study is entirely devoted to assortment decisions, while all the other marketing decision variables are disregarded.

The most basic function in marketing is sorting. There are other functions in marketing such as transportation, storage, credit, display and promotion. But sorting is the decision aspect of marketing whether seen from the standpoint of the supplier or the consumer. ... While the marketing specialist is interested in all of the transformations which take place as goods move to market ..., his most vital concern is with the sorts intervening between successive transformations. (Alderson 1965, p. 34.)

Furthermore, changes of assortment policies do generally take place gradually, and the time span of the data collection of this study is short (less than one year - see Section 3.6). This means that the enterprise cannot conceivably have undertaken such great changes in its price, distribution, advertising and other marketing policies that the assortment policy has been altered. The enterprise also confirms this notion.

Hence, we conclude:

(b) The study is oriented exclusively towards assortment decisions, i.e., the other parameters of the firm's marketing mix are considered extraneous.

Within a reseller enterprise, assortment decisions are made at different planning levels, e.g., at strategic, tactical and operational levels. Strategic assortment decisions are of such far-reaching and complex character that the actually affect the question of what industry the seller is in. The include decisions whether to engage in new product groups and abandon existing ones (Swinnen 1982, p. 49-50). Tactical decisions, or management control, involve issues of assortment depth and breadth, price and quality levels, market segment adaptation and related matters. In the tactical planning, decisions concern the products and items within the product groups which are strategically settled. Operational plannig, finally, consists of the specific tasks of executing the product decisions made at the tactical level. (Anthony 1965.)

As this study deals with the decision criteria applied in the management's choice of products for the assortment, it is limited to the tactical or management control level of the planning hierarchy. The tactical decisions are made within the framework of various strategic issues, which concern business philosophy, organizational structure, assortment policy, etc. (Swinnen 1982, p. 66.) All these higher level decisions are regarded as constant conditions and external factors. As the study comprises one enterprise during a short period of time, this approach can be justified. This does not, however, mean that strategic issues are unimportant. On the contrary, to be able to interpret the findings of the study, it is necessary to relate them to various preconditions, and among them, the enterprise's strategic position is vital. Hence, a detailed presentation of the enterprise's characteristics is imperative. (See Section 3.2.) The operational issues of assortment planning within the enterprise are, on the other hand, of no interest for this study.

So, the conclusion is:

(c) The study is restricted to criteria applied in decisions concerning assortment issues at the tactical or management control level, while strategic issues are considered as constant, and operational planning is irrelevant.

Assortment decisions are always made inside certain organizational structures, both internal ones within the organization and external ones, describing the organization's relations to suppliers and other actors. Within these organizational structures, there are various processes, which are related to or affect the assortment decisions - information exchange, interpretation and evaluation of information, identification of alternatives, negotiations, decision rules, etc. To combine all these activities and the relevant organizational structures, we can use the concept of "assortment building function." It is a subfunction of the total marketing or distribution function. (Alderson 1965, p. 35.)

Thus, we conclude:

(d) As this study is focused on assortment decision criteria, it should be understood that only a minor part of the assortment building function of the firm is investigated. All other issues within this function are considered external and constant.

As mentioned above, assortment decisions are very important marketing decision parameters. In spite of this, assortment decisions receive only scant treatment in the scientific marketing literature. Compared to pricing, advertising, personal selling and several other marketing variables, knowledge of assortment composition is quite limited. There are, actually, only a few researchers who are trying to reach a theoretical understanding of assortment building.

It might be impossible to prove this assertion, but some indications can be given:

- In a random sample of eight recent elementary textbooks on marketing, assortments (product mix, product lines etc.) are treated on six pages on average, while the corresponding figure for price policy is 32 pages, for advertising 21 pages, personal selling 21 pages and physical distribution 11 pages.
- In a typical year, the Marketing Abstracts section of the Journal of Marketing seldom reports more than five articles on assortment issues, while there are some 50 articles on advertising, between 10 and 20 on personal selling and about 10 on pricing.
- According to lists of American doctoral dissertations compiled by University Microfilms International (1982) and by the American Marketing Association (1977-1982), there is only one dissertation on assortment issues every second year. Advertising issues are studied in eight to fourteen dissertations per year, personal selling in four to five, pricing in two to three and physical distribution in two, all approximate figures.

1.3   The Concept of Assortment Decisions

During the last one or two decades, research on organizational buying has evolved as one of the most expansive branches of the marketing discipline. Within this body of literature, the are also many contributions to an understanding of reseller assortment building. As a reseller company composes its assortment, it is making numerous decisions concerning purchases from suppliers.

When trying to apply generalizations about organizational buying in general to reseller assortment decisions in particular, there are two provisos, which are discussed below. One concerns the object for the decisions, i.e., all assortment decisions are not buying decisions. The other concerns the decision maker's identity, i.e., reseller companies may deviate from the type of organizations treated in the organizational buying behavior literature. The first problem is discussed in this section, the second one in the next section.

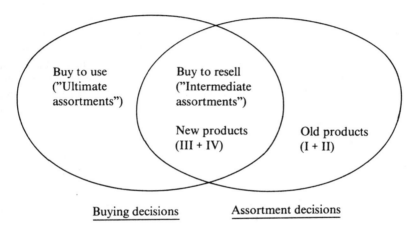

Figure 1-1: Buying Versus Assortment Decisions

Assortment decisions and buying decisions cannot be claimed to be identical entities. Firstly, many buying decisions concern products which the buyer intends to use in his production or his consumption, and, if the narrow assortment definition is used (see Section 1.1), these have nothing to do with any assortment. According to the extended assortment definition, they should, however, be termed assortment decisions. (See the upper half of Figure 1-1.)

Secondly, even if the buyer buys in order to resell, there is a divergence between assortment decisions and buying decisions, no matter which assortment definition is used. Assortment decisions constitute a more comprehensive group than buying decisions, i.e., all buying decisions are assortment decisions, while the opposite is not true. (See the lower half of Figure 1-1.) Buying decisions concern the question of whether new products should be accepted or rejected (Categories III and IV in Figure 1-2). There are, however, also assortment decisions dealing with whether existing products should be retained or deleted (Categories I and II). These cannot reasonably be called buying decisions, though in many cases, i.e., in changes, they are related to buying decisions.

This leads us to the following statement:

(e)   As this study treats criteria used in assortment decisions, it includes both decisions on new products (acceptance/rejection) and decisions on old products (retention/deletion). Both types of decisions influence the composition of the reseller's assortment, hence, they should be considered as being of equal importance.

The object of the assortment decision is an assortment, and the purpose is to rearrange that assortment in such a way, that a new, but similar, assortment is composed as advantageously as possible, in terms of the reseller's objectives. (Cf. Alderson 1965, pp. 84 and 132 on "The potency of assortments.") The assortment decision can be regarded as consisting of a number of subdecisions, one for each of the products involved, new as well as old. As there are cost and demand relations between all products within the same assortment, all decisions are interdependent, and in principle, they must be made simultaneously. The decision maker must base his decision on various information about all the products concerned.

Hence, the assortment decision concerns how, among the total set of products (I+II+III+IV in Figure 1-2), to arrange a new assortment (I+III), replacing the previous one (I+II). This implies that an assortment decision is a

Decision outcome / Class of products	Positive decision outcome	Negative decision outcome
Old products	I (Retention)	II (Deletion)
New products	III (Acceptance)	IV (Rejection)

After decision / Before decision	Within assortment	Outside assortment
Within assortment	I	II
Outside assortment	III	IV

Figure 1-2: Classification of Assortment Decisions - Two Versions with Identical Contents.

complex system, with a large number of interdependent product decisions as constituent elements.

(f) The interplay between the various product decisions making up an assortment decision, as well as their concomitant complexity and simultaneity should be taken into account in the design of the study. (It might, though, for technical reasons, be necessary to make some simplifications.)

The object of the buying decision is one or a number of new products. Hence, the perspective becomes more restricted. The purpose is not to redesign an assortment as optimal, but to select the best possible product to include in the assortment. The complex interrelations between all the products of the assortment decision become considerably simplified in the buying decision. Normally, several subdecisions are not made simultaneously; usually it is a matter of one decision on whether a new product should be accepted or rejected. (III versus IV in Figure 1-2.)

Old product decisions (retention/deletion) and new product decisions (acceptance/rejection) differ in some basic respects. These have important implications for the entire assortment building process.

Firstly, the information bases for old and for new product decisions are not the same. Stated simply, the decision makers have good *a priori* knowledge in cases of old product decisions, but bad *a priori* knowledge when it concerns new product decisions. It is true that in all assortment decisions, it is the future sales and profits potentials of the products which are crucial, hence, there are always forecasts, no matter whether it concerns old products or new ones. The bases for these forecasts are, however, very different for the two decision types.

For an old product, there is a host of facts - sales statistics, experiences of various kinds within the reseller organization, etc. - and all these can be used for the predictions. For a new product, on the other hand, there is no inside-organization information but only the supplier's sales presentation, observations of competing resellers' eventual handling of the product and similar uncertain information. Neither the consumers nor the store personnel are acquainted with the product; the way it affects the sales of other products is unknown, etc. All this means that the forecasts must necessarily be based on a great deal of guesswork. The conclusion is that new product decisions are bound to be more uncertain and risky than old product decisions.

Secondly, there are differences between old and new product decisions which are due to the fact that the consequences of incorrect decisions differ widely. If sales and profits of a product would develop positively, this product should be retained (if old) or accepted (if new), and similarly, the product should be deleted or rejected, if the product's development would be negative. ("Ideal situation" in Figure 1-3.) It is, however, unavoidable that the decision makers sometimes reach faulty conclusions, whereby they delete and reject products which actually have good prospects and retain and accept products which fail ("Mistake" in Figure 1-3).

Decision consequences / *Decision outcome*	The product's performance is/will be/would be ...	
	... satisfactory	... unsatisfactory
I *Retention* **Old products**	Ideal situation	Mistake! The product can, however, be deleted later with only minor losses due to the delay. The mistake is easily discovered: Good *a posteriori* knowledge
II *Deletion*	Mistake! Large losses occur in lost sales, in selling out old stock, and possibly also in reintroducing the product. The mistake is difficult to discover: Poor *a posteriori* knowledge	Ideal situation
III *Acceptance* **New products**	Ideal situation	Mistake! Large losses occur in market introduction and then in selling out the stock. The mistake is easily discovered: Good *a posteriori* knowledge.
IV *Rejection*	Mistake! The product can, however, be accepted later with only minor losses (lost sales) due to the delay The mistake is difficult to discover: Poor *a posteriori* knowledge	Ideal situation

Figure 1-3: Consequences of Different Decision Outcomes.

Different mistakes have very different consequences. With regard to old products, a faulty retention decision can be corrected later without any serious problems, while a faulty deletion decision is both difficult to remedy and quite costly. For new products, the situation is reversed. A faulty acceptance decision gives large losses, though it can be quickly changed, while a faulty rejection decision is fairly unproblematic.

Thirdly, there are differences as to the decision makers' *a posteriori* knowledge, i. e., their ability to evaluate the correctness of their decisions afterwards. In decisions leading to retentions or acceptances it is easy to follow the products' sales and profits records, as the products are in the assortment. This means that, if a poor product has been accepted or retained, the decision makers' mistake will soon be discovered. In deletion and rejection decisions, one can only guess how the product would have developed. So, if a good product is deleted or rejected, the decision makers may never find out that they have made a faulty decision, as the product is out of their sight.

These observations lead to a number of conclusions, all of which indicate a general pattern: retention and rejection decisions (I and IV) greatly outnumber deletion and acceptance decisions (II and III):

- The first and most important is, of course, that there are important differences between old product decisions and new product decisions. Not only do the decision makers have to base their deliberations on very different kinds of information, but there are also differences as to the consequences of the decision outcomes.
- The above-mentioned differences between retention and deletion decisions and between acceptance and rejection decisions in cases of incorrect forecasts lead to a conservative attitude among the decision makers. In uncertain situations it is wise to maintain the status quo. Unless the decision makers feel fairly secure, it is rational for them to retain old products rather than delete them and to reject new products rather than accept them. There is a kind of inertia built into the system.
- In old product decisions this inertia is reinforced by the fact that the negative consequences of a faulty deletion decision are very pronounced. The losses may be significant, especially as they include some lost sales, and such a decision is in practice quite irreversible. Hence, it is understandable that decision makers hesitate to delete their old products.
- In new product decisions there are two mechanisms which add to this inertia. 1) The uncertainty due to insufficient information will make the decision makers more cautious about acceptances. 2) The fact that faulty rejection decisions are probably never discovered means that some potentially good products are not included in the assortment.
- Though these tendencies are inherent in all assortment decision making and of general validity for all resellers, there are differences in degree, due to the fact that various situational factors cause the magnitude of the negative consequences of faulty decisions to vary. For example, some reseller may have administrative routines that make the reversal of faulty decisions slower than others. Some may have an organizational set-up that causes the losses from faulty decisions to become come greater than in other firms. Some may have such poor communication systems that they can hardly identify the mistakes they have made.

1.4   Organizational Types

Having shown in the preceding section that there is a certain overlap between the two concepts of (organizational) buying decisions and assortment decisions, we will here discuss to what extent current knowledge of organizational buying behavior is applicable to the study of reseller assortment decision criteria.

The main part of the research within the field of organizational buying consists of studies of industrial, i.e., manufacturers', buying. Research on resellers' and public authorities' buying is, actually, very limited. In most cases, however, the researchers do not distinguish between these types of organization in their reports. For example, findings concerning government and reseller buying are presented under the heading of "industrial buying," and more commonly, the researchers use the term "organizational buying" when they actually base themselves on studies of industrial buying only. (See, e.g., Webster & Wind 1972, Hill & Hillier 1977 and Johnston 1981.) The three types of organization are, in other words, treated as one. Knowledge, attained from one type, is uncritically considered valid also for the other two.

This is not to say that there are no similarities between the three types of organization. There are, of course, just as there are some parallels between consumer and organizational buying. (See the various articles in Consumer and Industrial Buying Behavior 1977.) But generalizing from one type of organization to another, without stopping to examine whether it is reasonable to do so, entails a risk of false conclusions. The differences between the conditions of the three types of organization are so great, that marked differences between their buying procedures and buying organizations should be expected.

Hence, there are, among others, the following general differences between manufacturers and resellers, which are bound to lead to numerous and important differences between the buying decisions of these two types of organization:

- Resellers buy in order to resell; manufacturers buy to use the products in their production.
- Need analyses and motives are simpler in the reseller company than in the manufacturer company.
- The assortment function in the reseller company comprises a larger number of decisions per unit of time than is the case in the manufacturer.
- The economic consequences of the average buying decision are lesser for the reseller than for the manufacturer.
- In the reseller company a buying decision can be revoked quickly and simply, but this is generally not so in the manufacturer company.
- The reseller can routinize its assortment function to a higher degree than the manufacturer.

- For the reseller assortment decision making is a specialized responsibility, while many and various officials take part in the manufacturer's buying decision process.
- Reseller companies are generally in a stronger position with regard to their suppliers than most manufacturer companies are.

Between public authorities, on the one hand, and reseller and manufacturer companies, on the other, there are generally even greater differences regarding the prerequisites for buying decisions. The most decisive difference is that a public authority deals with various kinds of citizen services on the basis of a politically settled goal, while the two types of companies most often have a profitability goal. From this follow several divergences, for example, concerning organizational structure, choice of suppliers and customers, decision criteria and information handling procedures.

So, the difference between the buying function within the three types of organization might, perhaps, be so great, that one should follow Mallen's suggestion and use different concepts:

If the consumer is the buyer, then that side of the act is termed shopping; if the manufacturer, purchasing; if the government, procurement; and if a retailer, buying. (Mallen 1969, p. 177.)

The conclusion that emerges from this discussion is the following:

(g) The possibilities of using existing knowledge about manufacturers' and public authorities' purchasing in the design of this study are considered quite limited, as resellers differ from these two organizational types in fundamental respects. The generalizations, which might be made, must be held at such a high level of abstraction, that they become trivial. On the other hand, it is, of course, of utmost importance that existing knowledge about reseller buying criteria is utilized as far as possible in this study.

This also means that we do not think that the findings of this study can be transferred to manufacturers and public organizations. To what extent they are valid for other resellers is hard to say, as we do not know how representative the enterprise studied is for resellers in general. At a higher level of abstraction it is, however, evident that several lessons can be learned about reseller assortment decisions in general.

This discussion can be carried a step further: one can question whether there are any systematic differences between assortment decisions in different types of reseller companies, for example, wholesalers and retailers. No definitive answer can be given, but there are probably certain differences, as wholesalers and retailers do not operate under the same conditions. We consider, however, these differences to be fairly small and of a type where the variables are the same, while the variable values differ.

Another interesting question concerns the interplay between the various levels of the distribution channel. Evidently, the assortment decision criteria applied by the channel members at one level have repercussions on the criteria applied at other levels of the channel. As all the channel members are interdependent, each one has to take the others' goals and criteria into consideration, when settling his own criteria. This means that, in a study of, for example, wholesaler decision criteria, it might be relevant also to include the manufacturers', the retailers' and perhaps the consumers' product choice criteria.

Such an all-encompassing study would, however, hardly be feasible. Nor is so broad a perspective required for the basis of the present study:

(h)   The study is limited to the assortment decision criteria on only one level of the distribution channel, the central wholesale level, while the other channel levels, i.e., manufacturers, regional warehouses, stores and consumers are regarded as constant, external factors.

Because of the short time span for the data collection, it is improbable that the actors within the other channel levels have changed their assortment decision criteria so radically that the criteria of the central wholesale level have been affected.

1.5   The Concept of Decision Criteria

The focus of this study is the concept of criteria. The aim of the study is to contribute to our knowledge of the criteria which determine resellers' assortment decisions.

It might be conceived as ideal, if one could identify an absolutely general model of criteria, which could explain all reseller assortment decisions, irrespective of organization, industry, product group and other circumstances - if one could produce an exhaustive list of criteria and determine the relative importance of each. As will be shown below, such an ambition is, however, unrealistic. Actually, which criteria a decision maker applies are always a consequence of a multitude of situational factors.

This is not to say that a general list of criteria cannot be produced. It can, for certain, but it must then be expressed in such aggregate terms, that it will not be able to explain or predict specific decision cases. Rather, it could only serve as an overview.

Criteria, choice criteria, evaluative criteria and decision criteria are all identical concepts. The one who chooses among alternatives must evaluate these in certain respects - according to certain criteria - and this evaluation results in a decision whereby one of the alternatives is preferred. It can also be seen that there is a direct parallel between the criteria and the attributes of the alternatives. When evaluating a product (or anything else), one identifies certain of its attributes. Which attributes are seen, is determined by what is considered to be important for the product, and the attributes are important, because they, in one way or another, contribute to the decision maker's goal attainment.

Criteria are a specific type of goal. As the decision maker chooses one alternative rather than others, he expects that the chosen alternative contributes to the attainment of a superior goal, for example, welfare, profitability or power position, better than alternatives which are discarded. Hence, the criteria are subordinate to this goal - they are subgoals in relation to this. As the criteria are used for guidance in concrete action, they are operationalizations of a superior goal, and, as such, very far-reaching. The criteria can thus be deduced from goals at high levels in the decision maker's goal hierarchy. Ultimately, they originate in the goal at the very top of the goal hierarchy, and they are themselves located at the very bottom.

The fact that the criteria derive from a superior goal does not, however, mean that it is possible to determine a number of criteria on the basis of a certain goal high up in the hierarchy. Each goal can be attained in many alternative ways. There are many strategies to reach the superior goal, and each strategy implies second-rank goals, which in turn can be reached in different ways. One can continue in this way throughout the goal hierarchy. Which of the alternative subgoals best satisfies the higher-level goal - irrespective of levels in the hierarchy - depends on various circumstances of the decision maker and his environment.

This means that the superior goal sets the parameters of variation for other goals and criteria. (Simon 1973 and Kast 1974.) There can be no criteria which do not fit the superior goal, as they are, ultimately, derived from this. The criteria are a way to attain the superior goal, but each set of criteria is only one way among a very large number of alternative ways.

The reseller assortment choice criteria are subordinate to the organization's top goal. Let us suppose that we have a traditional profit-oriented company, i.e., that profitability is the superior goal. Then the criteria used in all company decisions - not only assortment decisions, but also decisions concerning advertising, personnel policy, machine investments etc. - aim at furthering its profitability. Profits can, however, be attained in different ways. For one company, a policy with a limited assortment of lowpriced goods, sold with minimal service, might be the best route, while another could prefer the opposite policy.

Which policy is best is determined by a variety of internal and external factors. Among the internal ones can be mentioned the company's capital structure, its assets in buildings and equipment, the know-how of its officers and the visions and philosophy of the owners and the managers. External factors are, among others, the competitive situation, the customers' price and service sensitivities, the supply of goods and services and the actions of the authorities.

This leads to the following conclusion:

(i)   Although an exhaustive classification of reseller assortment decision criteria would, no doubt, be very useful, there would be little point in attempting a systematic assessment of each and every criterion. Rather, research effort should be directed towards the search for various patterns and the identification of different typical situations. What is interesting is finding out how various internal and external conditions influence decision criteria, not merely identifying these criteria. To gain more profound insights, it is necessary to explain why different criteria are applied in different situations, and that requires that the identified criteria are related to various situational factors, expressing organization attributes and decision types as well as environmental traits.

Hence, we expect to find that different criteria are applied in different types of decisions, depending on the specific circumstances prevailing for these decision types. For example, one might wonder what it means for the reseller's choice of criteria that the company is large or small, that it has many distributor brands or few, that the supplier is predominant or marginal, etc.

The situational dependency of decision criteria is very pronounced in consumer behavior theory. For example, there is a distinct difference between the consumer's choice of stores and her choice of products. In the former case the heterogeneity of the decision situation is less, and therefore, it is possible to identify a fairly invariable set of criteria, while such a general list of criteria cannot exist in product decisions. (Engel & Blackwell 1982, pp. 418-421 and 519-528.) Furthermore, there are differences between high and low involvement decisions. For the former, the consumer uses more numerous and more specified criteria than for the latter. (Engel & Blackwell 1982, pp. 23-38.) It may be hypothesized that a similar relation exists in reseller buying, i.e., that important decisions require a larger number of and more elaborate criteria than less important ones. (Cf. Swinnen 1983, pp. 125-128.)

In the organizational buying literature there are also some propositions on how the choice criteria are related to various situational factors. Mostly, they regard this type of decision as a bundle of situational factors, e.g., the classification into straight rebuy, modified rebuy and new buy. (Robinson, Faris & Wind 1967.) Nevertheless, there is a considerable amount of research still to be done.

The identified decision criteria do generally express nothing or very little about the "background" factors. If one, in a realistic way, presupposes that the reseller companies, because of their varying situational and environmental conditions, do not exhibit any homogeneous buying behavior, the influence relations of the independent variable groups should be examined and, on this basis, concrete statements should be reached about the behavioral relevance of each of the variables. (Sauer 1982a, p. 77. Our translation.)

In other words, a "contingency approach" should be applied in this study. (See, for example, Kast & Rosenzweig 1973, pp. vii-xi, and Kast & Rosenzweig 1974, pp. 505-518.) This means a recognition of complexity, variety and situational dependency, and it implies that all understanding is relative to and dependent on a number of environmental factors. Hence, one should realize that somewhat different decision criteria are used in different assortment decisions. Therefore, it is not sufficient merely to identify which criteria are used, but one should also study the circumstances in which they are used and, finally, try to explain how the identified criteria are related to the various situational factors.

1.6 Aim and Design of the Study

The conclusions, (a) to (i), in the preceding sections can now be summarized in a more elaborate statement of the aim and the design of the study:

The study seeks, through an empirical analysis, to contribute to a general understanding of assortment decision criteria in reseller companies. The empirical work deals with the criteria, applied at the central wholesale level of a highly integrated grocery chain, in its decisions regarding the composition of the assortment offered to the regional wholesale level and the retail level of the chain (a). An assortment decision consists of a number of subdecisions concerning new and old products (addition and deletion decisions) (e), which are interrelated in a complex system (f). The aim of the study is to include every conceivable variety of criteria and to explain why different sets of criteria are important under different circumstances (i).

The research work is based on a few simplifying presumptions:

- The assortment decisions are unrelated to the other marketing decision parameters (b).
- The assortment decisions are found at the tactical planning level (c).
- The assortment decision criteria can be studied independently of other issues concerning the company's assortment building function (d).
- The assortment decision criteria of reseller companies deviate from those of other organizational types (g).
- The assortment decision criteria at the wholesale level are considered as independent of those at other levels of the distribution channel (h).

2 LITERATURE SURVEY

2.1 Outline of the Chapter

The present chapter continues the discussion on the theoretical bases of the study, though at a more specific level than in the preceding one. In Chapter 1, quite general theoretical issues were treated, so that we, from a basic and broad point of departure, gradually could delineate the subject and, finally, arrive at a specification of the aim of the study. This chapter comprises analyses of the previous research within the thus defined problem area.

The ultimate purpose of the study has been stated as a contribution to our knowledge of reseller assortment decision criteria. In the following is presented a survey of existing knowledge within this area. Hence, this chapter describes the theoretical foundation on which the study could be based, and which could serve as the point of departure for conclusions about its further design as well as which results of previous research should be expanded on. Finally, this chapter could also serve as a general state-of-the-art review within the subject area.

This introductory section (2.1) gives an overall picture of the scope, the origin and the character of previous research. Section 2.2 proceeds with deeper characterizations of the previous research projects, as seen from the perspectives of this study, i.e., structured according to conclusions (a) - (i) of Chapter 1. Then, Section 2.3 discusses the possibilities of combining and classifying the components of our present knowledge, followed by a general classification of decision criteria. Based on this structure, Section 2.4 presents a comprehensive review of the findings of the previous research dealing with reseller assortment decision criteria. Furthermore, to this chapter is linked Appendix B, which reviews 34 previous studies, noting, in particular, the lists of criteria at which they arrive.

Evidently, the phenomenon of reseller assortment decision criteria is very old - just as old as trade itself. As long as there have been merchants, there have also been assortments for sale, and the merchants must always have had certain criteria for how their assortments should be composed. As an object for research, reseller assortment decision criteria are, of course, considerably younger, but nevertheless - in relation to many other branches of business administration research - it is comparatively old. For example, Grashof (1968, pp. 25-27) presents some books from the beginning of this century, where various purchasing decision criteria are discussed and evaluated.

It is, however, only within the last 25-30 years, that systematic research on reseller assortment decision criteria has been conducted. Today, at least 34 reports can be found. (See Appendix B.) This number might seem remarkably large, but it includes several studies which are quite small and simple - for example, those conducted by certain trade magazines (Graf 1968, Mueller & Graf 1968, Coops & Voluntaries 1974, Lebensmittel-Zeitung 1970 and 1975, Progressive Grocer 1978 and others) - as well as some studies, where the question of decision criteria is only subordinate (e.g., Kihlstedt 1961, Davidson, Doody & Sweeney 1975, Gripsrud & Olsen 1975 and Hutt 1975). By far most of the studies - more than half - originate from the USA, but research has also been conducted in Canada, the United Kingdom, West Germany, Belgium, Norway, Sweden, Finland and France.

Looking only at the years of publication, it seems that research interest has come in waves. Four periods can be identified, during which reports of somewhat different character have been published. It should, however, be recognized that the time of publication is an inadequate indicator, as the research itself could have been conducted several years earlier.

The first wave occurred around the first half of the 1960's, and it consisted of a number of minor studies, containing only enumerations of decision criteria. (Nigut 1958, Gordon 1961, Hileman & Rosenstein 1961, McNeill 1962, Food Trade Marketing Council 1964a and 1964b, Einstein 1965.) Among these were articles where the authors called attention to the fact that changes in industry structure were bringing new roles to the resellers, so their assortment decisions and criteria were becoming more significant for the manufacturers. All in all, however, these studies were quite limited, with only exploratory and descriptive purposes.

The next wave came in the end of the 1960's, when several larger works with a more ambitious approach were published (Borden 1968, Grashof 1968, Berens 1969 and 1971/72, Hix 1972). It was common to all of these that the authors tried to present comprehensive and elaborated treatments of the subject of reseller assortment building, including the decision criteria as one part. These studies were, however, still oriented towards describing and detailing the constituent elements of the subject area, rather than trying to explain or build theoretical frameworks.

Towards the mid 70's a number of reports were published with great variations in scope and purpose. (Among others, Doyle & Weinberg 1973, Heeler, Kearney and Mehaffey 1973, Sweitzer 1974, Arora 1975, Montgomery 1975, Johnson 1976, Lindqvist 1976.) Some of these studies present methods for examining decision criteria. In others, the study of criteria entered as a subtopic within a more comprehensive problem area. Nevertheless, the reports of this third wave indicate that the development of knowledge concerning reseller assortment decision criteria had passed beyond the merely exploratory level.

The fourth wave started in 1980, and (hopefully) is still going on. (Bauer 1980, Douglas 1980, Nilsson 1980, Sauer 1982a and 1982b, Swinnen 1982 and

1983.) The descriptive purposes have now given way to more comprehensive approaches, with the aim of attaining understanding and explanations. Hence, these are extensive studies, though relatively few in number.

The preceding account should make it clear that previous research represents a truly diversified mixture. The studies differ widely in scope, aim and approach. More than one third of the studies are doctoral dissertations; one fifth are articles in scientific journals and about as many are articles in trade magazines; some are reports from trade organizations, consultant agencies etc.

Most of these studies, by far, are empirical research. Among the larger reports, there is actually only one that is not based on primary empirical data but solely on other literature. (Bauer 1980.) On the other hand, it contains excellent literature surveys and develops highly perceptive theoretical considerations.

In conclusion, it must be said that the development of knowledge concerning reseller assortment decision criteria has been very slow and groping. It is true that numerous studies have been conducted in the course of the last three decades, but, in general, these have had such a restricted perspective that their contributions to a more profound theoretical understanding of the problem area are small. Only a few large-scale and thorough analyses have been made, to be found mainly in the studies of the "fourth wave." With due recognition, the total knowledge of reseller assortment decision criteria must, nevertheless, be considered as quite insufficient.

2.2   Characterization of Previous Research

In this section, previous research is characterized in a number of respects, relevant to the present study, namely in relation to positions (a) to (i), explicated in Section 1.1 to 1.5. By the same token, these positions are also characterized in relation to the present state of knowledge. Positions (a), (b), (c) and (h) prove to be in close accord with previous research. There is fair, but not perfect congruity on (d) and (i). Finally, there is considerable divergence on positions (e), (f) and (g).

(a)   Perspective and purpose (See Section 1.1.)
With few exceptions, the empirical studies use, just as this study, the resellers' own situation as their point of departure. Most of the studies are based on data attained from the resellers, even though various data sources are used - written and personal interviews with buyers, managers, committee members etc. as well as analyses of different types of documents. Only three studies collect data from outside sources, mainly from the suppliers to the trade. (Hix 1972, Kaiser

(not published, but, according to Bauer 1980, conducted 1975), Angelmar & Pras 1984.)

The vast majority of studies are conducted without any explicit vested interest. Rather, it seems to be the researcher's general, personal interest, that has governed his work - a purely scientific endeavor. This does, however, not preclude that the researchers often state that their findings could be of practical value, either for resellers or for suppliers.

Those studies which have an explicitly expressed vested interest, are generally smaller. Among these, it is far more common that the researchers want to help the resellers raise the effectiveness of their assortment building functions than they try to assist the suppliers in achieving more effective marketing.

(b)   Assortment decisions versus other marketing decision parameters (See Section 1.2.)

The present study is based on the simplifying assumption that assortment decisions can be regarded as unrelated to other marketing decisions of the reseller. All the previous studies, considered here, make the same simplification, at least in those parts which concern assortment decision criteria.

(c)   Assortment decisions at the tactical planning level (See Section 1.2.)

Also in this respect, there seems to be complete agreement among the various studies.

(d)   Decision criteria within the assortment building function (See Section 1.2.)

Several of the studies treat reseller assortment decision criteria and nothing else. (E.g., Hix 1974, Montgomery 1975.) It is more common, however, that the decision criteria constitute only a part of the object of research, but if so, they are generally the most important subproblem of the study. (E.g., Borden 1968, Grashof 1968 and Nilsson 1980.) For those studying the entire assortment building function of the resellers, assortment choice criteria must necessarily take a prominent position. Only a few studies treat the criteria as subordinate - for example, use the criteria as an instrument for analysis of buyer-seller interaction or as means of elaborating decision rules. (E.g., Doyle & Weinberg 1973, Hutt 1975 and 1979 and Sweitzer 1974.)

(e)   New and old products (See Section 1.3.)

Assortment decisions are either addition decisions (whether new products are to be included in the assortment) or deletion decisions (whether old products are to be excluded). For this study, the two decision types are of equal interest.

In previous research, however, it is by far most commonly the case that interest is directed solely at addition decisions and that deletions are not mentioned with one single word. The opposite, i.e., examination of deletion decisions only, is not found in any study. A few studies treat both addition and deletion decisions, but in these cases the former category is given considerably higher priority. (Borden 1968, Grashof 1968, Nilsson 1980, Swinnen 1983.) Only one study investigates deletion decisions so thoroughly that separate lists of criteria are presented for the two decision types. (Grashof 1968, pp. 68-72 and pp. 78-79.)

We can only speculate about the reasons for this remarkably skewed interest in addition and deletion decisions. One explanation might be that the researchers consider addition decisions to be more interesting, as they have greater importance for all involved parties - for the resellers themselves, for the suppliers, for the consumers and for society at large. Furthermore, it might be that deletion decisions are conceived of as simple and unproblematic, while purchasing decisions are more complex and abstruse. (Swinnen 1983, p. 81.) Likewise, it might be that it is more challenging, exciting and prestigeous working with new products than with old. The result, in any case, is one-sided knowledge and this is also pointed out by some researchers: "It should also appear useful to study the other side of the coin, product deletion decisions." (Montgomery 1975, p. 264.)

(f)   Interaction between product decisions (See Section 1.3.)
In paragraph (e), it was stated that very few studies treat both new and old products. Hence, there are also very few studies where it is possible to make more thorough analyses of the interdependence between acceptance and deletion decisions. Nevertheless, some reports do mention such interrelations in passing.

Likewise, interrelations may exist between different acceptance decisions and between different deletion decisions. The latter type of relations are very seldom identified. (Swinnen 1983, p. 54 and p. 286.) Interactions between acceptance decisions are found implicitly in certain discussions of some studies (e.g., Berens 1969). They are, though, not subjected to any thorough analyses in themselves.

The relations between different product decisions discussed in previous research are mainly of the following types:

- Several authors mention that, in the reseller's deliberations concerning new products, it matters considerably whether there already are similar products in the assortment. If the new procuct is significantly new or "unique," the probability for acceptance is high. (E.g., Grashof 1968, p. 70, Arora 1975, p. 93, Hutt 1975, Montgomery 1975, p. 256, Johnson 1976, pp. 33-36.)
  - The propensity to accept a new product is highly influenced by whether the

reseller already has products from the same supplier and by the reseller's experience with that supplier's current products. (E.g., Food Trade Marketing Council 1964a, Berens 1969, Doyle & Weinberg 1973, Arora 1975, Hutt 1975 and 1979, Johnson 1976.)

- Many resellers regularly conduct reviews of the assortment composition within various product groups, whereby a number of old products is deleted. Quite often, it is new product decisions, which give rise to such reviews - when analysing the prospects for the new products, the decision makers discover that the product group has some old products with inadequate records. (Hileman & Rosenstein 1961, pp. 54-55, Grashof 1968, pp. 75-76, Johnson 1976, pp. 24-26 and Nilsson 1980, p. 174.)
- The probability that a new product will be accepted is significantly increased if a corresponding old product can be deleted simultaneously. (Nilsson 1980, p. 174 and Swinnen 1983, pp. 290-294.) The resellers often apply a principle of "one in, one out." This is due to the fact that resellers generally must actively strive to keep their assortments restricted.

When studying assortment decisions, the decision outcomes can be conceived in two alternative ways: *either* the outcome is that a product is accepted or rejected, *or* the outcome is that the assortment becomes changed in a certain way. The difference is whether the specific product or the entire assortment is considered as the object of decision. From what has been said above, it is clear that the former perspective dominates strongly in previous research.

(g)   Generalizations (See Section 1.4.)
By far, the greatest part of previous research consists of descriptions of criteria, applied by various resellers under specific and given circumstances. This dominant approach gives no reason to doubt the specific validity of the studies, but, on the other hand, their generality is very limited.

The fact that the studies are generally only descriptive means, firstly, that their bibliographical relevance is minimal. More than half of the studies do not include any literature survey whatsoever. Less than one fourth of the studies have fairly thorough analyses of the previous research - mainly those published in recent years (the "fourth wave").

Secondly, the descriptive character of the studies means that the possibilities of applying their results to other resellers' assortment decisions are very limited. The findings may be valid for the specific companies studied, but probably not for others with other characteristics and in other circumstances. The question of generalizing the validity of the findings is, moreover, discussed in extremely few studies.

(h)   Distribution channel (See Section 1.4.)
The type of industry studied is highly skewed. All the empirical studies, except

five, are conducted in the grocery industry, just as the present one. Among the five exceptions are two studies of men's wear stores. (Berens 1969 and Hix 1972. Furthermore Kihlstedt 1961, McNeill 1962 and Angelmar & Pras 1984.)

Likewise, there is a marked skewness in the researchers' choice of distribution channel level. The most common, by far, is the central wholesale level of retail chains - again a parallel to this study. (E.g., Borden 1968, Johnson 1976, Lindqvist 1976 and Nilsson 1980.) In a few cases, independent wholesalers are studied. (Heeler, Kearney & Mehaffey 1973, Hutt 1975 and Douglas 1980.) Only seven studies treat the assortment decisions of retail stores, and among these are the two studies within the men's wear industry. (Also Kihlstedt 1961, Sauer 1982a and others.) It is remarkable that not one single study discusses whether the assortment decisions at the different levels of the distribution channel could be interrelated, and these are not examined. Nor are they in the present study.

(i)   Contingency approach (See Section 1.5.)

Several reports mention that different sets of criteria are applied in different situations. There might be differences between resellers, between buyers, between product groups, between suppliers etc. (Swinnen 1983, p. 69; Shipley 1985, pp. 34-35.) In some of these studies the researcher also tries to identify explanations of the differences found.

- Berens found that the two buyers studied applied different criteria, because they had widely varying professional backgrounds. (Berens 1969, p. 30.) Likewise, there turned out to be differences between the store, investigated in depth, and a sample of other stores; and these differences were claimed to be due to the very specific business policy of the store in question. (Berens 1969, p. 126.) Finally, there were differences between the criteria applied in different product groups, but these were not explained. (Berens 1969, pp. 168-173.)
- In Sweitzer's study, the buyers were found to apply different criteria, in some cases also very divergent. There was, however, no attempt to explain these. (Sweitzer 1974.)
- Arora identified fourteen decision criteria. "Each criterion was found to be most important in the decision-making concerning at least one new product." On the other hand, he did not find any significant differences between the criteria applied by different buyers. Nevertheless, Arora's observation led him to propose further research on how the relative weight of the criteria varies with product categories and with reseller type. (Arora 1975, pp. 112, 117-118.)
- Montgomery shows, in his so-called "gate-keeping" analysis, that the criteria for deciding whether a new product will be accepted or not, are

dependent on the characteristics of the product. (Montgomery 1975, pp. 261-263.)

- In a literature survey, Nilsson identified some differences between the decision criteria presented in European and in American studies, and he proposed that these might depend on "the size of the market, degree of concentration in the food distribution industry, functioning of business life, and cultural and historical backgrounds." (Nilsson 1977. See also Nilsson 1976.)
- Douglas found that the decision criteria vary with suppliers and supplier brand, which would depend on various characteristics of the supplier and the product. (Douglas 1980, pp. 212-228.) There were also differences between different types of distributors, but these were not subjected to analysis.
- The two resellers studied by Nilsson were found to apply partly different decision criteria. Analyses showed that these differences could be explained by the fact that the resellers represent different types of vertical marketing systems. (Nilsson 1980, pp. 133-135.)

In order to attain a deeper understanding of reseller assortment decision criteria, it is not sufficient to know which criteria are applied and with what weight. It is also necessary to understand why these criteria are important. That kind of understanding is strongly emphasized in the present study. Previous research shows that such an understanding can be attained in different ways.

Some authors give such thorough accounts of the resellers' total assortment building functions, that the reader gets an intuitive comprehension of the roles of the various decision criteria. (Borden 1968, Grashof 1968, Johnson 1976 and Bauer 1980.)

Another way to reach an understanding is to identify various categories of criteria and try to explain the differences by the use of some background variables. As mentioned above, such more or less detailed analyses are found in several studies. It is mainly this approach that is used in the present study.

Sauer represents a third and still more ambitious approach. He constructs a model analytically, showing how the decision criteria are affected by various characteristics of the reseller, the buying organization, the organizational members, the suppliers, etc. (Sauer 1982a, p. 124.) Finally, part of this model is tested empirically.

More than half of the studies have, however, no explanatory ambitions; they are solely descriptive. Hence, they consist of lists of criteria, applied in a number of specific situations, and in some cases, a ranking or weighting of these criteria. Why the criteria are used and are more or less important, is not explained in these studies.

2.3 Systematization

As the preceding section shows, the literature on reseller assortment decision criteria consists mainly of a large number of empirical studies, delineating what criteria have been used under various, specific conditions. This leads, automatically, to the thought that it might be possible to deduce a deeper and more generally valid knowledge within this subject area on the basis of all these listed criteria. This thought is pursued in this and the next section, where different types of insights are discussed:

a) Identification of a generally valid list of all conceivable criteria.
b) Determination of the relative importance of the various criteria, in a general sense.
c) Compilation of the findings of the various studies together with a discussion of how the criteria are related to one another and to various environmental factors.

The presentation is structured in the following way. First a few words are devoted to the difficulties associated with attempts to attain theoretical understanding on the basis of the previous research. Then follow presentations of two earlier studies' attempts to compile and generalize current knowledge within this subject area. The section concludes with our suggestion of how a general list of the decision criteria can be structured and, hence, serve as a basis for the empirical part of this study. Thus, having discussed points a and b above, point c is deferred to the next section, as this requires rather comprehensive treatment.

Deducing more general knowledge from the previous research is a very complicated task. The reason for this is that it is hard to see what the research results really show - what the concepts cover and what the objects of study are. (Similar observations are made by Arora 1975, p. 76, Sauer 1982a, pp. 77-78, McGoldrick & Douglas 1983, pp. 13-14, Swinnen 1983, pp. 17 and 83, and Angelmar & Pras 1984, p. 228.)

Firstly, the conceptual frameworks lack uniformity. Only a few authors present definitions of their criteria. In most cases, however, it is possible to grasp the meaning of the criteria, even though it is sometimes quite vague - for example, whether "price" means purchasing price or selling price. One and the same term can also have different significations, and it is often difficult to determine which one is intended. Furthermore, the authors express their criteria on different levels of aggregation (Bauer 1980, p. 283, footnote 1): while one author may have only one criterion for discounts, another, for example, might distinguish between five types of discounts. Finally, the researchers only seldom base their lists of criteria on those from previous studies. There is only one single case where one researcher uses identically the same criteria as another. (Thompson used the same questionnaire as Sweitzer 1974 - see Appendix B.)

Secondly, the studies deal with assortment decisions in different reseller organizations, each with its own specific conditions. To be able to interpret the findings - to understand why the criteria are assigned a certain weight and why they are identified at all - requires some knowledge about the various background factors of the decision making, for example, how the assortment building function is organized in the reseller enterprise, how the decision makers' information channels work, how the buyers make their product choices and how the product groups are composed. Facts about such situational variables, capable of explaining the criteria, occur, however, very sparsely in the research reports. (Cf. Section 2.2, Paragraph i.)

Hence, for the most part, previous research consists of isolated, empirical descriptions of the criteria used by various resellers, and it is conducted on weak theoretical bases. The literature yields numerous lists of criteria, but these are not only unrelated to one another, they are also often contradictory. The researchers identify different criteria, use different and incomparable definitions or - most often - no definitions at all, and generally also refrain from presenting the characteristics of their objects of study.

The conclusion to be drawn from this is that any attempt to identify patterns in previous research must contend with considerable uncertainties. This does not, however, prevent such attempts or make them undesirable. When deducing a more general pattern from the existing lists of criteria, these must be taken "at face value." All lists must be considered as equally valid, and the criteria must be interpreted as faithfully and reasonably as possible, i.e., if two authors use identical or similar terms for their criteria, these must be considered as meaning the same thing.

In the literature, there are a few attempts to attain more general knowledge on the basis of the lists of criteria from previous research reports. Especially the attempts by Bauer and by Nilsson should be mentioned, as these cover all the three points, a - c, mentioned above. They attack the problem, however, from quite opposite points of departure. (Bauer 1980 and Nilsson 1980.)

Bauer presents a very comprehensive and elaborated analysis of the subject. The presentation follows an analytical deductive approach. Based on general social science theories - economic theory, distribution theory, management theory, decision theory, etc. - Bauer conducts a series of logical argumentations, which leads to certain conclusions about assortment decision criteria. (Bauer 1980, pp. 226-281.) In this way, he identifies a large number of criteria, and, through his chains of reasoning, he also shows how the criteria are linked to one another and to certain situational factors. Appendix B gives a summary of Bauer's discussion.

The analysis continues with a survey of the findings from twelve empirical

Rank	Criterion	Nigut 1958	Food...FTMC 1964b	Nielsen 1968	Graf 1968	LZ 1969	Sweitzer 1974	Arora 1975	Hutt 1975	Kaiser 1975	LZ 1975	Heeler & al 1973	Montgomery 1975	Times mentioned	Average of relative rank
1	Competition with distributor brands												x	1	0.058
2	Introductory price					x								1	0.132
3	Product category growth potential												x	1	0.174
4	Profit potential	x					x	x			x			4	0.227
5	Consumer price					x				x	x			4	0.286
6	Advertising (+ Promotions)	x	x	x	x	x	x	x	x	x	x	x	x	12	0.312
7	Consumer value	x		x	x	x	x	x		x	x			8	0.384
8	Back-order guarantee												x	1	0.406
9	Sales quantity for special allowances						x							1	0.406
10	Retail incentives	x												1	0.406
11	Consumer demand	x	x	x	x			x		x				7	0.429
12	Competitors carry the item		x					x					x	3	0.434
13	Newness	x						x	x					4	0.459
14	Broker												x	1	0.464
15	Sales potential	x					x	x		x	x			5	0.490
16	Reputation of manufacturer				x				x	x				4	0.494
17	Timing of introduction and marketing	x					x	x						3	0.494
18	Time discount on payables											x		1	0.500
19	Manufacturer has regional stock						x							1	0.522
20	Special allowances				x									1	0.528
21	Rate of turnover for similar products						x	x						2	0.529
22	Growth of product category										x		x	2	0.566
23	Distribution												x	1	0.580
24	Introductory allowances		x	x	x		x	x					x	6	0.590
25	Product quality and appearance	x		x		x					x		x	5	0.598

Rank	Criterion	Nigut 1958	Food...FTMC 1964b	Nielsen 1968	Graf 1968	LZ 1969	Sweitzer 1974	Arora 1975	Hutt 1975	Kaiser 1975	LZ 1975	Heeler & al 1973	Montgomery 1975	Times mentioned	Average of relative rank
26	Advertising and promotion allowances	x	x				x	x	x					5	0.606
27	Seasonality	x					x	x						3	0.619
28	Test market results	x		x					x				x	4	0.632
29	Way of calculating conditions						x	x						2	0.661
30	Package size	x	x								x			3	0.669
31	Package design	x					x	x	x	x	x		x	7	0.684
32	Individual sales promotion						x							1	0.696
33	Sales presentation									x			x	2	0.718
34	Gross margin					x				x	x	x	x	5	0.759
35	Shelf space			x			x	x					x	4	0.764
36	Number of substitutes carried								x		x	x		3	0.770
37	Display material			x		x					x			3	0.782
38	Reliability of manufacturer	x								x				2	0.790
39	Customer traffic in stores	x												1	0.870
40	Cash discount			x										1	0.875
41	Type of sales promotion measures				x	x						x		3	0.927
42	Recommended price					x								1	1.000
43	Delivery time						x							1	1.000
44	In conflict with company policy	x												1	1.000

Figure 2-1: Bauer's Summary of New Product Decision Criteria, Suggested by Twelve Studies (Source: Bauer 1980, p. 310. Our translation.)

studies of reseller assortment decision criteria, all with rankings of the criteria. (Bauer 1980, pp. 282-313.) All the criteria mentioned in these studies are thereby shown to have parallels among the deductively identified criteria. The latter also comprise several criteria not mentioned in any of the empirical studies.

The analysis concludes with an attempt to derive the relative importance of the criteria from the twelve empirical studies (corresponding to point b above). The first stage of this is to reduce all the criteria to a list of 44 criteria (or categories of criteria). For each criterion a quotient is then calculated, expressing this criterion's rank in relation to the rank of the least important criterion in the same study. Finally, averages are computed for all the criteria within the same category. In this way, the relative importance of all the criteria mentioned in the twelve studies is combined in a new, aggregate list of criteria. (See Figure 2-1.)

In this list of 44 criteria there are, however, some which are found in only one study, and it is questionable how reliable these are. To analyse this problem, Bauer presents four alternative lists, with additional requirements that the criteria should be mentioned in at least three, four, five and six of the empirical studies, respectively. (See Figure 2-2.)

Ranking of criteria mentioned in at least 6 of the 12 studies	Ranking of criteria mentioned in at least 5 of the 12 studies	Ranking of criteria mentioned in at least 4 of the 12 studies	Ranking of criteria mentioned in at least 3 of the 12 studies
		1. Profit potential	1. Profit potential
		2. Consumer price	2. Consumer price
1. Advertising (+ promotions)	1. Advertising (+ promotions)	3. Advertising (+ promotions)	3. Advertising (+ promotions)
2. Consumer value	2. Consumer value	4. Consumer value	4. Consumer value
3. Consumer demand	3. Consumer demand	5. Consumer demand	5. Consumer demand
			6. Competitors carry the item
		6. Newness	7. Newness
	4. Sales potential	7. Sales potential	8. Sales potential
		8. Reputation of manufacturer	9. Reputation of manufacturer

4. Introductory allowances	5. Introductory allowances	9. Introductory allowances	10. Timing of introduction and marketing
	6. Product quality and apperance	10. Product quality and apperance	11. Introductory allowances
	7. Advertising and promotion allowances	11. Advertising and promotion allowances	12. Product quality and apperance
			13. Advertising and promotion allowances
			14. Seasonality
		12. Test market results	15. Test market results
			16. Package size
5. Package design	8. Package design	13. Package design	17. Package design
	9. Gross margin	14. Gross margin	18. Gross margin
		15. Shelf space	19. Shelf space
			20. Number of substitutes carried
			21. Display material
			22. Type of sales promotion measures

Figure 2-2: Bauer's Ranking of New Product Decision Criteria, Mentioned in Twelve Studies, According to Number of Times Mentioned. (Source: Bauer 1980, p. 311. Our translation.)

Nilsson's approach is, in a certain respect, quite the contrary of Bauer's. (Nilsson 1980, pp. 62-87.) In his attempt to construct a generally valid list of decision criteria, Nilsson first selects ten empirical studies. The criteria included in these are arranged in a number of categories, so that each criterion is allocated to one single category. The result is a systematization with ten main categories and a total of 25 subcategories.

The classification of decision criteria is as follows (rearranged here):

A. Profitability and sales (Evalution of the product's future profits and sales prospects)
   A1   Overall profitability
   A2   Rate of turnover
   A3   Sales potential

B. Economic conditions (The various economic conditions in the agreement between supplier and reseller)
   B1   Supplier's price
   B2   Gross margin
   B3   Allowances and rebates
   B4   Support to cooperative advertising
   B5   Credit terms
   B6   Other economic conditions

C. Assortment considerations (The product's relations to other products of the assortment)
   C1   Existence of distributor brands
   C2   Relations to other products

D. Consumer evaluation (Factors indicating the consumer's conscious and subconscious appreciation of the product)
   D1   Overall consumer value
   D2   Retail price
   D3   Product's physical characteristics
   D4   Product's psychological characteristics
   D5   Packaging

E. Supplier marketing (The supplier's stake of various marketing measures)
   E1   Introductory marketing campaign
   E2   Continual marketing

F. Supplier characteristics (Factors directly related to supplier identity, i.e., policies, resources, organization, etc.)
   F1   Supplier representative
   F2   Reputation and reliability
   F3   Sales force organization
   F4   Services and functions
   F5   Other characteristics

G. Competitive considerations (References to the assortment building of other resellers)

H. Distributive factors (The product's degree of adaptation to the physical distribution system)

I. Tactical considerations (Deliberations about the short and long term implications of the power relations to the suppliers)

J. Salesman presentation (The supplier representative's personal influence)

The next step in Nilsson's systematization is analysis of the interrelations between the categories of criteria. The procedure here is deductive and fairly simple. Nilsson makes logical assumptions that imply certain connections between the criteria. In this way, he reaches a structure that is hierarchical, rather than systemic. (See Figure 2-3.)

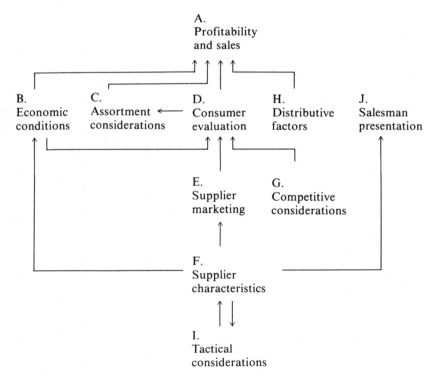

Figure 2-3: Nilsson's Hypothesized Pattern of Interrelations between Decision Criteria (Source: Nilsson 1980, p. 69. Our translation.)

It should also be mentioned that Nilsson's literature survey is the basis for an empirical study, where, among other things the relations between the criteria are examined. In doing so, the deductively established structure proves to be too crude a simplification. In reality, many more interrelations can be identified - so many that they cannot be mapped hierarchically. Instead, they form a system, which is best visualized by a matrix. (See Figure 2-4.) (See Swinnen 1983, pp. 102-105 for a more systematic analysis of interdependence of criteria.)

This reasoning leads to the conclusion that the most important and most frequently used criteria are profitability and sales, economic conditions, consumer evaluation, supplier marketing and supplier characteristics. The empirical study gives rise, however, to certain distinctions:

- *Profitability and sales* are the ultimate, decisive criterion, hence, they are always of great importance for the decision outcomes.
- To assess the sales prospects of the item, the decision makers base themselves mainly on *supplier characteristics, consumer evaluations* and *economic conditions,* hence, these criteria are most often very influential.
- In many cases, the *supplier's introductory marketing campaign* and *assortment considerations* might be important.
- *Tactical considerations* in the choice of supplier have a bearing only in certain cases, but then they may be wholly decisive.
- *Distributive factors, salesman presentations* and *competitive considerations* seldom have any importance. (Nilsson 1980, p. 166. Our translation.)

Independent variable \ Dependent variable	A	B	C	D	E	F	G	H	I	J
A. Profitability and sales										
B. Economic conditions	x			x		x				
C. Assortment considerations	x					x		x		
D. Consumer evaluations	x		x							
E. Marketing					x					
F. Supplier characteristics		x	x	x	x				x	x
G. Competitive considerations		x		x						
H. Distributive factors	x	x	x							
I. Tactical considerations		x	x			x				
J. Salesman presentation						x	x			

Figure 2-4: Nilsson's Identified Pattern of Interrelations between Decision Criteria (Source: Nilsson 1980, p. 165. Our translation.)

This evaluation of the relative importance of the criteria is admittedly very crude and vague. This is, however, deliberate in recognition of the fact that the significance of the criteria varies, depending on what conditions are present in the concrete decision cases - a contingency viewpoint.

Evidently, the lists of criteria presented by Bauer and by Nilsson seem to be the most comprehensive and relevant ones. Some other authors also present lists which are well elaborated - mainly Grashof (1968), Arora (1975), Montgomery (1975) and Swinnen (1983).

The structure of criteria, proposed by Nilsson, with ten main categories and 25 subcategories, is chosen as a point of departure for the empirical part of this study. Firstly, this list is short and incisive, just as it is, presumedly, exhaustive. Secondly, it implies a contingency approach, which is well in accord with the bases of this study. Thirdly, it has, in Nilsson's study, proved itself to be operational in empirical work.

To check the generality and the usefulness of the list of criteria, we have made an attempt to classify all the 394 criteria which are mentioned in the studies presented in Appendix B. (Nilsson's study is not included, however, as it would be self-reinforcing.) The list is originally based on 113 criteria from ten studies. If it turns out that the additional criteria can be arranged in the structure without difficulties and that they are distributed over the various categories in about the same proportions as the earlier ones, we consider the usefulness of this categorization to be corroborated. This is also the case. (See Figure 2-5.)

With this classification of assortment decision criteria we have reached a conclusion with regard to point a in the introduction of this section. The next question is whether there are also some conclusions to be drawn regarding further work on point b, i.e., the relative weight of the criteria.

On the basis of a general theoretical discussion we concluded in Chapter 1 (Section 1.5, Paragraph i) that a contingency approach should constitute a point of departure for the study. This implies, among other things, that the importance of the criteria depends upon various situational factors, and hence, it is impossible to rank the criteria after their importance in a general way. We hold that the discussions earlier in this section support the correctness of our choice of a contingency approach as a basis for the study:

- The relative weight of the criteria varies extremely in previous empirical studies. The main reason for this must be that these studies deal with different objects, each with its own characteristics.
- Bauer makes a very comprehensive analysis, in order to determine the relative weight of criteria, but the result is quite disappointing. Firstly, the ranking varies strongly with the number of studies considered. Secondly, it is evident that the ranking is dependent upon which studies it is based on.

Category of criteria	Number of criteria, mentioned in previous studies according to	
	Nilsson 1980	This study
A. Profitability and sales	14 (12%)	50 (13%)
A1 Overall profitability	4 (4)	12 (3)
A2 Rate of turnover	2 (2)	7 (2)
A3 Sales potential	8 (7)	31 (8)
B. Economic conditions	23 (20%)	75 (19%)
B1 Supplier's price	2 (2)	6 (2)
B2 Gross margin	5 (4)	14 (4)
B3 Allowances and rebates	5 (4)	17 (4)
B4 Support to cooperative advertising	4 (4)	13 (3)
B5 Credit terms	3 (3)	7 (2)
B6 Other economic conditions	4 (4)	18 (5)
C. Assortment considerations	9 (8%)	21 (5%)
C1 Existence of private brands	2 (2)	3 (1)
C2 Relations to other products	7 (6)	18 (5)
D. Consumer evaluation	19 (17%)	75 (19%)
D1 Overall consumer value	4 (4)	20 (5)
D2 Retail price	3 (3)	11 (3)
D3 Product's physical characteristics	4 (4)	18 (5)
D4 Product's psychological characteristics	4 (4)	13 (3)
D5 Packaging	4 (4)	13 (3)
E. Supplier marketing	15 (13%)	51 (13%)
E1 Introductory marketing campaign	4 (4)	34 (9)
E2 Continual marketing	11 (10)	17 (4)
F. Supplier characteristics	20 (18%)	79 (20%)
F1 Supplier representative	3 (3)	5 (1)
F2 Reputation and reliability	8 (7)	30 (8)
F3 Sales force organization	2 (2)	5 (1)
F4 Services and functions	3 (3)	33 (8)
F5 Other characteristics	4 (4)	6 (2)
G. Competitive considerations	3 (3%)	13 (3%)
H. Distributive factors	5 (4%)	15 (4%)
H1 Transportation adaptation	2 (2)	4 (1)
H2 Store adaptation	3 (3)	11 (3)
I. Tactical considerations	2 (2%)	3 (1%)
J. Salesman presentation	3 (3%)	7 (2%)
	113 (100%)	394 (100%)

Figure 2-5: Classification of Assortment Decision Criteria

Thirdly, Bauer's rankings lack explanations which could link the criteria together and convey an understanding of them.
- Nilsson makes a simple attempt to assess the relative weight of the criteria on a theoretical basis. His conclusions are equivocal - and thus in line with the contingency approach. The empirical part of Nilsson's study leads to a similar conclusion, i.e., the importance of the criteria varies with various situational factors.

The conclusion is that we consider it impossible to determine the relative weight of the criteria in a general way on the basis of previous research (point b). Rather, our task in the empirical part of this study is to identify the importance of the various criteria and to relate them to some background factors, thereby obtaining explanations.

The next section presents an attempt to make a synthesis of the findings of previous research dealing with the various decision criteria (point c). The section is structured according to the classification presented above, with ten main categories of criteria.

2.4 State of Knowledge

A. *Profitability and Sales*
In some previous studies, it is explicitly stated that profitability is the ultimate criterion for the resellers' assortment decision. All other criteria serve as indicators of profitability, i.e., they are subgoals in relation to the profitability goal. (Gordon 1961, p. 59; Borden 1968, p. 203; Grashof 1968, p. 68 and 1970, p. 239; Bauer 1980, p. 229; Douglas 1980, p. 200; Nilsson 1980, p. 166; Douglas & McGoldrick 1981, p. 21; Sauer 1982a, p. 107; Swinnen 1983, p. 67 and p. 79; Shipley 1985, p. 27.) The subgoals which are most closely tied to profitability are sales and demand. In some other studies it is only implicit that profitability is a superior goal. The authors treat the various criteria as ways of increasing the volume of sales and profitability, and they seem to regard it as self-evident, and not worth a discussion, that profitability is the ultimate goal. (Hileman & Rosenstein 1961, p. 55; Nigut 1972, p. 60; Doyle & Weinberg 1973, p. 51.)

(Resellers) need to be sure that the product will improve their overall trading position, "that we will be better off with it than without it" and that they can make a profit on that particular deal. (Johnson 1976, p. 27.)

Proof of consumer demand for a new product is undoubtedly a first, important criterion of acceptance or rejection for all decision makers. ... Thus, we arrive at a group of criteria which can be regarded as indicators of the new product's chances of success and anticipated sales. (Bauer 1980, p. 229. Our translation.)

In practically all other studies, profitability and sales are considered on a par with other criteria, i.e., all criteria are treated as independent and on the same footing, and no superior goal is discussed. The results of these studies show, however, that quite often profitability and sales and similar criteria are among the most important ones. (Hix 1972, p. 63; Heeler et al. 1973, p. 37; Montgomery 1975, p. 259; Arora 1975, p. 113.)

From this, it can be concluded that previous research lends favorable support to the conception that profitability is the superior goal and the most important criterion for the assortment decisions. The relationship between profitability and the other criteria is, however, sparsely elucidated in the literature.

Profitability is, of course, highly dependent upon sales volume. What is decisive, however, is not the sales of the individual product but that of the entire product mix. There are strong interrelations between the sales potentials of the various products within the assortment. The sales volumes are, obviously, related to consumer acceptance of the products, but behind this, there are many explanatory variables, such as supplier reputation and marketing program. When evaluating the suppliers, one should also consider their delivery ability, cooperativeness, etc. The choice of supplier is also a question of great long-term importance; tactical considerations can thus be decisive. Besides sales volume, profitability also depends upon prices, agreements and various conditions in the supplier relation. Finally, one has to take into account how the products fit into the physical distribution system of the chain. (Nilsson 1980, pp. 166-167. Our translation.)

As the reseller has access to sales statistics for the products contained in the assortment, the sales criterion is considerably easier to apply in deletion decisions than in acceptance decisions. Hence, the predominant motive for deleting old products is low sales volume and a negative sales trend. (Gordon 1961, p. 59; Grashof 1968, pp. 78-79; Nilsson 1980, pp. 169-170; Swinnen 1983.)

The most important criterion in the evaluation of an item considered for deletion is its rate of sales, which is assumed to show consumer demand. Those products with a low level of consumer demand (rate of sales) are seriously considered for deletion ... In the majority of cases, deleting decisions are based on gross margin and unit movement data. (Grashof 1970, p. 240.)

Studying how the sales of a product are changing is easier than comparing its sales volume with that of other products. Hence, the sales trend of a product is often considered to be more significant than the figure for its sales volume. (Nilsson 1980, pp. 169-170. Our translation.)

One way to forecast the demand for a new product is to base the projection on the sales volumes of similar products in the product group. Parallel to this is the conception that product groups with growing sales should be expanded with more new items, while shrinking sales figures mean than the number of items should be reduced. (Swinnen 1983, p. 67.) Other forecasting bases are test sales results and supplier evaluations, and not least, the buyers' own estimates on the basis of product characteristics, marketing program, supplier market position, etc.

Since the new item will generally derive a majority of its sales from consumer substitution of the new item for other items, chains feel the present sales levels of these other items are reasonable indicators of the sales of the new item. Some of the other factors include the competitive reaction of the new item, test market information, and the estimated sales as presented by the supplier. The chains' informal estimate of sales then becomes one basis for the acceptance or rejection of the item. (Grashof 1970, p. 239.)

If a supplier can prove that the product is already selling well in other regions, types of stores, retailers etc. and/or that the market for the product category to which the new product belongs is expanding, this will influence the decision considerably towards acceptance. (Bauer 1980, p. 229. Our translation.)

In order to reach an appreciation of the sales potential of the new products, various factors are investigated, which in some way can influence sales results. Such are the supplier's marketing program, the price and the quality of the product, specific characteristics of the product, etc.... Other measures for helping the buyer to estimate a new product's sales potential are studies of sales trends, sales of competing retailers, consumer opinions and fashion. (Nilsson 1980, pp. 170-171. Our translation.)

The most reliable and most desirable measure of a new product's sales potential is the results of a sales test. (Johnson 1976, p. 22; Bauer 1980, pp. 229-230; Nilsson 1980, p. 171.)

Furthermore, the reseller often interpretes the fact that a manufacturer devotes resources to a sales test as a sign of the manufacturer's confidence in the product. This latter function of sales tests can have a significant impact on the resellers' attitudes.

B. Economic Conditions

The price of a product is important in two ways: it influences demand and sales volume, and it determines the gross margin of the reseller. (Bauer 1980, p. 260; Nilsson 1980, p. 193.) The two dimensions are of equal importance.

This means that the price criterion is of great and general importance. It is, however, mainly in cases where the price is remarkably high or low, that it is seen explicitly. A very high price can exclude a product from all further considerations, while a very low price can make a product interesting for the reseller, though not in itself decisive.

Thus, if the price is in the medium range, it is not always a critical variable; this is probably the reason why the price criterion is not very highly evaluated in most empirical studies.

The price at which a new product will sell in the stores is an important element in the total support mix; although a product would not be listed simply because it was very competitively priced, if the price is not right in the buyer's terms, it has very little chance of gaining access to the stores. (Johnson 1976, p. 72.)

The price of a product is, of course, evaluated in relation to the other products of the same product group. As to examining the sales potential of a product, the reseller also analyses the product's value for the consumer.

...suggested retail prices were usually compared to category prices; when they were found to be higher, the trade debated if it would hinder movements or they wondered how competitive supermarket firms might price them. There did not appear to be much concern on whether the prices represented an honest consumer value; perhaps the assumption was that current category prices were good values. (Borden 1968, p. 174.)

Buyers are looking for a product price that represents value for money to the consumer; they are also concerned, particularly in the present economic climate, that it should be in line with other products in its sector. (Johnson 1976, p. 72.)

There is also a rich array of other economic criteria: quantity discounts, bonuses, cash discounts, advertising allowances, introduction rebates, etc. So, the agreement conditions can vary considerably. As long as these conditions are within prevailing frameworks, they do not influence the decision outcomes significantly. If, on the other hand, they deviate from what is common, they can have a great impact; but in any case, such economic conditions can seldom induce a reseller to accept a product which is less satisfactory in other respects. (Swinnen 1983, pp. 95-96.)

Trade-oriented proposition elements, particular margins, buying allowances and terms of sale, were not very important elements in inducing acceptances. These elements were generally satisfactory when they corresponded with category norms and prior experience with the manufacturer. It seemed probable that margins and buying allowances that would violate (i.e. be under) established norms might not be acceptable. (Borden 1968, p. 213.)

The significance of the 'deal' in the decision to accept a new product varies according to the importance of the launch. Clearly, the greater the trade's reluctance to list a new product, the better the deal will have to be for it to gain a place in the supermarket. (Johnson 1976, p. 79.)

C.   *Assortment Considerations*
A number of studies mention that resellers face problems caused by the tendency of their assortments to expand too much, and for this reason, efforts to keep the assortments within reasonable bounds become an important factor in decision making. (Gripsrud & Olsen 1975, p. 31; Johnson 1976, pp. 12-13; Nilsson 1980, p. 172.) The motives for this attitude are cost considerations and lack of storage capacity in the retail outlets. It has, however, also been claimed that this is only an easy excuse for the resellers to turn down many new product proposals. (Hileman & Rosenstein 1961, p. 55; Johnson 1976, p. 12.)

In order to keep the assortment ranges within certain limits, the decision makers apply various principles. (Gordon 1961, pp. 58-59; Hileman & Rosenstein 1961, p. 54; Gripsrud & Olsen 1975, p. 14 and p. 50; Johnson 1976, pp. 24-26, 33 and 36; Bauer 1980, p. 231; Nilsson 1980, pp. 172-176.) They are generally restrictive towards new products. Most often they give high priority to products already in the assortment. They follow, to a great extent, the rule-of-thumb "one in, one out." (Swinnen 1983, p. 81.) They follow the sales development of the newly introduced products, in order to be able to delete them quickly again, if the trend is not satisfactory. They conduct special reviews of the assortments.

The basic attitude towards new products is thus often negative. It is, though, strongly dependent on the product character, and especially the product's degree of newness. Products with a low level of newness, such as variants of tastes, package sizes etc. (line extentions) and imitations of existing products (me too's), are seldom of any interest. (Johnson 1976, pp. 31-34; Bauer 1980, pp. 257-258; Nilsson 1980, p. 178; Swinnen 1983, p. 89.) Exceptions are made, if they offer other decisive advantages, like lower price, stronger marketing program or more reliable delivery.

New products are rarely given a warm reception by the grocery trade. Indeed, there were buyers who expressed a decidedly hostile view and declared themselves to be "opposed to new lines". (Johnson 1976, p. 12.)

The trade's attitude is more favorable towards products which constitute definite improvements compared to existing products, for example, regarding use or packaging. Furthermore, the trade readily tries new products which offer the consumer something new in any essential respect, such as convenience. In some product groups, it is even imperative that such products are accepted, as they make the assortment appealing to the consumer. Completely new products are, however, so rare that they are often met with scepticism and doubt by the buyers. On balance, it must be acknowledged that product newness is a rather important decision criterion. (Grashof 1968, pp. 143-144; Montgomery 1975, p. 261; Johnson 1976, pp. 38-48; Nilsson 1980, pp. 178-179.)

The first subjective criterion deals with the concept of the "newness" of the item and is used in the evaluation of the item offers. The use of the criterion is based on the assumption that chains must present an image of being modern and up-to-date to consumers. (Grashof 1968, p. 143.)

The so-called uniqueness of the products can be a decisive argument for the acceptance decision. Really new items should have an opportunity to prove their value, and the consumer should have a chance to decide whether the new products should stay in the assortment. By accepting new items the assortment becomes more exciting, while it would, in a competitive situation, be dangerous to neglect the unique items. (Nilsson 1980, p. 178. Our translation.)

Just as the reseller evaluates a product's degree of newness in relation to the other products of the assortment, all other characteristics of the product are compared to those of the current products. The product's role within the assortment is treated in several studies, and it is also said to be a very important factor. (*Inter al.* Gordon 1961; Hileman & Rosenstein 1961; McNeill 1962; Grashof 1968; Berens 1969; Heeler et al. 1973; Arora 1975; Bauer 1980; Nilsson 1980; Swinnen 1982 and 1983.) The expositions are, however, in general so short and vague, that it is unclear which interrelations are of importance.

The second important subjective criterion used by chains is the role of an item in the total mix of items stocked by the stores of the chain. The basis for the use of the criterion is the assumption that if a consumer is not satisfied by the mix of items carried by a chain she will switch to another store. A chain would, therefore, lose the profit of the customer on all items she might purchase. (Grashof 1968, p. 144.)

The second set of criteria results from the necessity of integrating the new product into a current assortment, where also type of store, shelf space and competitive situation must be taken into consideration. The adaption to the assortment and the possibility of deviating from the assortments of competitors, are the main factors. ... Furthermore, it is decisive how many substitute items there are in the assortment, how strong the substitutability is and what turnover these items have. (Bauer 1980, p. 231. Our translation.)

The reseller's distributor brands are normally given higher priority than products from outside suppliers. (Montgomery 1975; Johnson 1976, pp. 21-22; Lindqvist 1976; Nilsson 1980, pp. 175-176.) Nevertheless, the trade's propensity to support its own products seems to vary considerably.

Reviews of the assortments are sometimes made, both sporadically and systematically. (Hileman & Rosenstein 1961, p. 64; Gordon 1961, pp. 58-59; Johnson 1976, pp. 38-40; Nilsson 1980; p. 174.) Especially as the buyers contemplate the acceptance of new items, they become aware of old products, which are selling slowly, and which, therefore, should be expelled. (Swinnen 1983.) Systematic reviews are quite simple to conduct, as practically all resellers have computerized information systems, which can supply them with detailed sales statistics.

D.   Consumer Evaluation

An important step in the assessment of a product consists in estimating how the consumer regards the product and, thus, whether the consumer might be willing to buy it. Many of the previous studies report that the product's consumer value, the consumer's need for the product, the consumer's satisfaction and similar factors belong to the most crucial criteria. (*Inter al.* Gordon 1961; Grashof 1968; Berens 1969; Hix 1972; Nigut 1972; Sweitzer 1973; Arora 1975; Nilsson 1980.)

...the most important reason for stocking more than one brand was identified as being the desire to maximize customer demand. Again this factor was found to be a major consideration in the stocking of individual brands ... (Douglas 1980, p. 200.)

The procedures followed by the resellers to assess the consumer value of the products vary considerably. Some studies state that the buyers make evaluations of an almost intuitive nature.

The product itself, that is, the intrinsic qualities in taste, appearance and function, did not play a major role in trade decisions. (Borden 1968, p. 172.)
    The question of whether the new product offered a consumer value for the price was not an overt consideration in most trade evaluation. (Borden 1968, p. 173.)

According to other studies, the decision makers are much more analytical, try to single out various types of product characteristics and make more systematic evaluations and comparisons. In so doing, it is, to a remarkably high degree, price and various functional product characteristics that are considered, especially what is called quality. (See, for example, FTMC 1964a; Einstein 1965; Doyle & Weinberg 1973; Montgomery 1975; Johnson 1976; Lindqvist 1976; Nilsson 1980; Swinnen 1982.) Of the psychological characteristics, the product's degree of newness is given most consideration. (See, for example, Einstein 1965; Grashof 1968; Arora 1975; Lindqvist 1976; Nilsson 1980; Swinnen 1982.)

The ingredients that the trade are looking for in a new product are essentially:

i)   Real nutritional value;
ii)   Real increase in convenience;
iii)   Real improvement in economy;
iv)   A product-development offering a tangible benefit, either to the housewife, or the trader, or to both.

(Johnson 1976, p. 29.)

E.   Marketing

Most authors claim that the marketing campaigns, which the suppliers are planning in connection with their product launches, have great influence on the buying decision. Some studies even state that this factor is the most important one. (Hileman & Rosenstein 1961; Borden 1968; Graf 1968 and Mueller & Graf 1968; Grashof 1968; Arora 1975; Montgomery 1975 and others.) On the other hand, there are also studies which declare that the role of the introductory campaigns is insignificant. (Gordon 1961, p. 60.)

Consumer advertising and promotion were the most effective elements of the product proposition in securing supermarket acceptance and distribution. (Borden 1968, p. 174.)
    The first and foremost of the secondary criteria is the promotional program of the supplier. If the new item is being supported by a large, expensive promotional program, the chain will give a high estimate to the expected level of movement. The chain will be even more favorably impressed if, in addition to a strong national advertising program, a strong advertising program supported by couponing and/or sampling is to be conducted in the chain's local market. Further, chains respond to

guaranteed advertising programs rather than programs dependent upon distribution. (Grashof 1968, p. 68.)

Hence, the influence of marketing plans is not equally great in all cases. (Doyle & Weinberg 1973; Johnson 1976, pp. 67 - 72; Nilsson 1980, pp. 182-183; Swinnen 1982, p. 47.) It has been said that the introductory campaign can be decisive under certain circumstances, namely, if the marketing effort is very comprehensive, and if other factors are not conclusive. The introductory campaigns influence the position of the buyers in two ways: they give an indication of the supplier's own faith in the product, and they stimulate the consumer to test purchases.

The literature mentions several examples of cases where very extensive introductory campaigns forced the buyers to accept new products, since they did not dare to leave the stores without items for which marketing had created a great demand. (Borden 1968, p. 178.and others; Johnson 1976, p. 69.) For the buyers, however, it is unsatisfactory being pressed by the suppliers in this way. The relationship between the buyer and the supplier might thus be damaged.

Another issue where the various studies are fairly unanimous concerns the buyers' evaluations of the scope of the introductory campaigns. The buyers rarely make any sophisticated analysis of the campaign plans, such as an assessment of the advertising designs. Rather, they only ascertain that the campaign has a certain size. (Gordon 1961, p. 60; Borden 1968, p. 174; Johnson 1976, p. 71; Nilsson 1980, p. 184; Swinnen 1983, p. 91.)

The strength of advertising and promotion came in large measure from a combination of elements rather than the effectiveness of any single element. In the trades' quick evaluation it was a consumer program that was deemed effective; individual consumer elements of the program did not in and of themselves carry the decision. (Borden 1968, p. 174.)

F.   Supplier Characteristics

Several authors mention that buying decisions are influenced by which supplier is presenting the new product, and some even consider this factor to be the most crucial. (See, for example, Hileman & Rosenstein 1961, p. 55; Gripsrud & Olsen 1975; Lindqvist 1976; Douglas 1980.)

Trade attitudes favorable to the manufacturer were highly important to many sales by influencing perceptions of product propositions and more importantly, negating, in the trade's judgement, much reason for analysis of the proposition or application of criteria. (Borden 1968, p. 214.)

The single most important variable influencing the listing of a new product is the manufacturer behind it. The buyers acknowledge that they listen harder to some manufacturers than others; certainly the larger manufacturers with major brands in the sector into which the product is to be launched are assured of a very attentive hearing. (Johnson 1976, p. 54.)

According to Montgomery's gate-keeping analysis, the four or five most well-reputed suppliers of the industry are fairly sure of getting their new products accepted, provided the products are satisfactory in terms of newness and marketing. Similarly, poor and unknown suppliers have small chances, unless their products have a high degree of newness and heavy advertising support. Offers from suppliers with only moderately good reputations are more uncertain and are scrutinized in more detail. (Montgomery 1975.)

Likewise, the various Scandinavian studies report that supplier size is of tremendous importance for assortment decisions. Nevertheless, also average-sized and smaller suppliers have good chances of having their products accepted, if the reseller regards them as reliable. (Gripsrud & Olsen 1975, p. 50; Lindqvist 1976, p. 54; Nilsson 1980, p. 185.) It also occurs that suppliers are categorized, resulting in great differences in their chances of having their new products accepted. (Gripsrud & Olsen 1975, p. 14; Nilsson 1980, p. 186.)

While explaining the way in which the supplier's identity can influence the buyers' assessments, researchers mention various factors, which can be summarized in a concept of reliability. Of special importance are the size of the supplier (since market research and marketing ability are related to this), and the sales volumes of the supplier's current products (since these indicate the prospects of the new products). Other related factors are the supplier's service packages, production facilities, management, product policy and product development programs. (Brown & Purwar 1980; Swinnen 1983, p. 98.)

Trade attitudes appeared to be primarily a synthesis of many feelings and judgements that the trade had built up from prior experience with a manufacturer and his sales presentations ... Some of the experience that appeared to exert an influence on buyers' attitudes toward manufacturers offering new products were: Success with previous new product introductions; evidence that previous introductions were accompanied by adequate advertising and promotion support; satisfactory movement of products in distribution; position (share and reputation) of the manufacturers' brands in the market; evidence of advertising support on products in distribution; honesty and competence of direct sales representation; and store support by the retail sales force. (Borden 1968, p. 206.)

It came as no surprise to hear the trade say that they are more receptive to new lines from the major suppliers with a healthy track record of successful launches in the market in question ... Large suppliers have also established backup services to the trade (distribution, invoicing and so on) which will limit the administrative problems attached to accepting any new lines. (Johnson 1976, p. 58 and p. 60.)

These quotations should make it clear that the concept of supplier reliability has two main components, both of which are relevant for the reseller's profitability. (Davidson, Doody & Sweeney 1975, p. 382; Bauer 1980, p. 238.) One is the supplier's marketing capability, influencing the reseller's sales volume. The other is the supplier's way of conducting various services, which has implications for the reseller's work and thus for his costs.

G.   Competitive Considerations

Several reports mention that the resellers, in their assortment decisions, take the assortments and the buying decisions of competing trade into consideration. (FTMC 1964a; FTMC 1964b; Grashof 1968; Berens 1969; Nigut 1972; Heeler et al. 1973; Sweitzer 1974; Montgomery 1975; Nilsson 1980; Swinnen 1982.) Most of these state, however, that such competitive considerations belong to the least important criteria. (Montgomery 1975 is a clear exception.) The competitors are said to play an indirect role, to the extent that the consumers are influenced by competitor action, and it is consumer demand that is of interest.

If all of a chain's competition in a market are carrying an item, that chain is likely to believe it made a mistake in not accepting the item before, that consumer demand for the item does exist, and that they should add it to the list of items now stocked. (Grashof 1968, p. 64.)

H.   Distributive Factors

Factors of importance for the physical handling of the goods during transport and in the stores are mentioned by several authors. (FTMC 1964b; Graf 1968; Grashof 1968, pp. 71-73; Sweitzer 1974; Montgomery 1975; Bauer 1980, pp. 258-259; Nilsson 1980, pp. 197-198; Swinnen 1983, p. 100.) Generally, such factors seem, however, to have quite limited influence on the assortment decisions, unless it is a question of extremely bad offers.

A product could come in such a large consumer package that there would hardly be room for it on the store shelves. A store package could comprise so many consumer packages that the smaller stores could not handle it, and they could not sell all the items within a reasonable period of time. (Nilsson 1980, p. 198. Our translation.)

I.   Tactical Considerations

The question of whether resellers take tactical angles into consideration in their choice of suppliers is closely related to the degree of concentration and integration in the trade. It is therefore readily understood that this issue is discussed mainly in studies on Scandinavia, where three or four retail congromerates dominate about 90 percent of the supermarket trade. (Lindqvist 1976 and Nilsson 1980. See also Arora 1975, p. 94 and Bauer 1980, p. 239 ff.) Resellers have the capability and a reason to take tactical actions against suppliers, only if they have superior power over them.

   Tactical measures are most often directed towards large and market-dominating suppliers. The reseller can, for example, actively support minor suppliers, suddenly break off the trade relation to a supplier, boycott a supplier for a few years, shift between different suppliers in different years, etc. (Lindqvist 1976, pp. 81 and 87; Nilsson 1980, p. 191.)

J. Salesman Presentation

Some studies deal with the way assortment decisions are affected by the manner in which the product is presented by the supplier's representative.

Their findings, however, are strongly contradictory. Most of them say that the seller has very limited ability to influence the decision outcome. (FTMC 1964a; Borden 1968, pp. 189-191; Hix 1972; Montgomery 1974; Johnson 1976; Nilsson 1980, pp. 198-199.) The two studies which analyse this question in most detail do, however, show that a good salesman presentation has a favorable influence on both the buyer's recommendation to the assortment committee and the committee's final decision. (Graf 1968; Arora 1975, pp. 95-107.)

3 EMPIRICAL BASES

3.1 Outline of the Chapter

In the first two chapters, we have presented the theoretical foundations of our study. The present chapter deals with its empirical basis. Section 3.2 provides a description of the enterprise studied, especially the assortment building function of its central wholesale level. The two subsequent sections treat the enterprise's goal and criteria: Section 3.3. discusses the concept of consumer interest as the ultimate goal of the organization as a consumer cooperative business, while Section 3.4 recounts its assortment decision criteria according to a previous study. In Section 3.5, data sources are discussed, especially the data source used in this study, viz., the forms which the buyers regularly present to the assortment committee. The process, scope and structure of the data collection are described in Section 3.6. Finally, Section 3.7 presents the variables, based on the above-mentioned data source, which are used in the study.

It should be mentioned that one of the authors has conducted an earlier study of the same enterprise's assortment building function during the same period. (Nilsson 1980.) There are, however, some fundamental differences between that study and the present one. The former study had a much broader perspective. It included, beside the enterprise studied here, also its main competitor, thus incorporating an important comparative approach. Furthermore, it comprised all aspects of assortment building, which means that the decision criteria constituted only a part of the study, though an important one. The former study also used a very different type of methodology, viz., a purely qualitative approach with data collection through participant observation and data analysis through the socalled "constant comparative method." (Glaser & Strauss 1967.)

As the preceding study and the present one differ widely in perspective and methods, no complete concordance between the results of the two studies can be expected. In fact, to some extent even different types of results are obtained. Nevertheless, if the two studies are able to complement each other, there would be an advantage in the synergic effect. Studying a phenomenon from different angles generally gives an opportunity for a more precise as well as a deeper understanding of the phenomenon. This research approach is often called triangulation. (Jick 1979.)

The desire to elicit a triangulation effect is the reason why the findings from the earlier study of the enterprise's decision criteria are delineated in Section

3.4. The knowledge gained from that study is not only relevant for Chapter 5's interpretations of the results of the present study; it can also facilitate an understanding of the discussions on the design of this study, especially the choice of the data source in Section 3.5 and the formulation of variables in Section 3.7.

3.2 Description of the Enterprise

The following description of the enterprise includes both facts which give a general background for understanding the empirical study as a whole as well as the various methodological choices, and facts which can serve as explanatory variables in discussions of the situational dependence of the decision criteria to be identified in the study. In the present context, the enterprise in question is of interest solely as the source of empirical data which can support broader generalizations on assortment building criteria. So, it matters little that the description of the organization as of 1975 is no longer valid today, and that the data set is dated. (Indeed, for this very reason it is no longer so confidential; and this has the advantage of easier access.) In the years which have passed, so many changes have taken place in the enterprise that the findings are no longer valid for its assortment building.

The empirical study is based on data which have been attained from Kooperativa Förbundet (KF) in Stockholm, which is the Swedish union of consumer cooperatives. KF is the apex organization for 188 consumer cooperatives with a total of about 1.8 million households as members.

The consumer cooperatives vary immensely in size. The largest association, with its 387 outlets, accounts for one fifth of the chain's total retail gross revenue; the ten largest count for two thirds; the 25 largest count for 85 percent. Hence, most of the cooperatives are very small, running only one or two stores.

Within the consumer cooperative movement, there are stores of widely varying types: hypermarkets, department stores, supermarkets, superettes, etc. In all, there are 2,358 retail outlets with a total gross revenue of about 13 billion Swedish kronor. (See Figure 3-1.) The cooperatives' share of the population's total private consumption is 8.5 percent, the market share of retail goods in the narrow sense is 18.1 percent; the market share of food is 21.2 percent.

KF performs a large number of distribution functions on behalf of the consumer cooperatives, such as assortment building, storage, marketing, personnel training, financial aid, economic consultation and many others. Hence, KF serves as a wholesaler in relation to the associations and their stores. By far the largest part of the supply of goods to the associations originates from KF and its regional warehouses.

Furthermore, KF owns a large number of factories, but it also contracts production among many independent manufacturers. This means that a

Type of retail outlet	Number	Gross revenue (million Skr.)	Gross revenue per outlet (million Skr.)	Share of food	Share of non food	Share of restaurant
Hypermarkets	17	1372 (11%)	81	44%	53%	3%
Department stores	166	5287 (41%)	32	46%	50%	4%
Supermarkets	212	1602 (12%)	8	80%	20%	0%
Superettes	1810	4346 (34%)	2	82%	18%	0%
Separate restaurants	72	90 (1%)	1	0%	0%	100%
Other outlets (busses, specialty goods stores, etc.)	81	235 (2%)	-	-	-	-
Sum	2358	12932				

Figure 3-1: The Retail Store Structure of the Consumer Cooperatives

relatively large part of the assortment consists of products sold as distributor brands. Some of the largest of its own factories are found in the following areas:

- canned and frozen vegetables and meat and fish products;
- beer and soft drinks;
- fresh meat and processed meat products;
- coffee and spices;
- margarine and ice cream;
- chocolate and candy;
- bread and cereals.

The Swedish cooperative movement is characterized by a very high degree of vertical integration. It is true that the cooperative associations are autonomous, but the economic relationships between the associations, the warehouses and regions, and the central level are so close and interdependent, that the cooperatives appear almost as a corporate marketing system.

The cooperatives are organized in 15 regions. The stores within each region are served by a single warehouse, except for two regions, where each has two warehouses. There is also one so-called central warehouse, located outside Stockholm, which supplies the cooperatives of the entire country with goods having a very low rate of turnover.

At the warehouses there are buyers, whose task is to compose the regional assortments out of the total assortment, which is determined by KF headquarters. They also make supplementary purchases of some fresh goods from local suppliers. The store managers then select goods from the warehouse assortments for the assortments of their stores.

The total assortment comprises slightly more than 5000 items. One eighth of these are at the central warehouse, and the rest are at all or some of the 17 regional warehouses. Of the 4300 items of the regional warehouses, two thirds are food items, while the rest is non-food. In the central warehouse, non-food items are preponderant.

The size of the total assortment increases slightly, with one or two percent annually, i.e., with 50 to 100 items. The non-food sector is growing more than the food items. In one year, 500-700 new products are added to the assortment, while 500-600 are deleted. Less than half of all the offers from the suppliers are accepted.

The task of composing the total assortment is carried out by nearly 200 buyers and an assortment commmitte. It also happens quite often that other departments of the enterprise are consulted, mainly the test kitchen, with its consumer panel, and the food laboratory. The buyers work with the assortment cases in all phases of the decision process, except for the very last

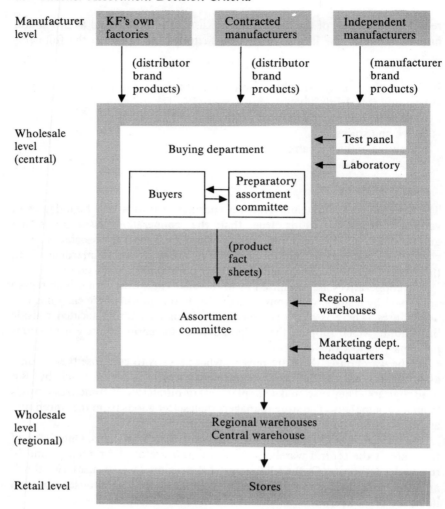

Figure 3-2: KF's Assortment Building

one. The final and formal decision is in the hands of the assortment committee. (See Figure 3-2.)

The buyer receives an offer from the supplier, collects information about the consumer market, competition, physical distribution possibilities, analyses the product's prospects in relation to the assortment, negotiates with the supplier, etc. Finally, he gathers all the factual results of his analyses in a so-called product fact sheet, adding his own proposal for decision. The product fact sheet provides room for data about the new product's sales forecast, the sales trends of current products, prices, etc. (See Figure 3-3.) The product fact sheet

Buying department: Date: Product: Number:

OFFERS

Product:	Supplier:	Net weight/: volume	Lowest sales price:	Price per unit:	Delivery time:	Com-: ments
....	....	....	....	....	....	....
....	....	....	....	....	....	....
....	....	....	....	....	....	....
....	....	....	....	....	....	....

PRODUCTS IN ASSORTMENT

Product:	Supplier:	Net weight/ volume:	Lowest sales price:	Price per: unit	Quantity sold, consumer packages	Store classification	Warehouses
....	....	....	....	....	....	....	....
....	....	....	....	....	....	....	....
....	....	....	....	....	....	....	....
....	....	....	....	....	....	....	....

THE BUYING DEPARTMENT'S PROPOSALS

Product:	Add:	Delete:	Net weight/ volume	Estimated yearly sales:	Store classification	Retail price:	Committee decision
....	....	....	....	....	....	....	....
....	....	....	....	....	....	....	....
....	....	....	....	....	....	....	....
....	....	....	....	....	....	....	....

Marketing action:
Other information:

Buying department representative:

Figure 3-3: KF's Product Fact Sheet

is then sent to the assortment committee members, for whom it is the main
basis for decision. Most often, the committee decides in accordance with the
recommendation given by the buyer on the product fact sheet.

With few exceptions, each buyer is responsible for all the products within a given assortment section, which comprises a number of related product groups. This means that the buyers deal with all three product sources: KF's own factories, the contract manufacturers and the independent suppliers. Hence, the buyers are not only buyers of manufacturer brand products but also product managers for the distributor brand products. The buyers are located at the KF manufacturing plants, which means that the central assortment building function is organizationally and geographically very decentralized.

Being a product manager for the distributor brands is a considerably more demanding and varied task than making purchases from outside suppliers. This means that the buyers who are responsible for many distributor brand products have smaller assortment sections, i.e., fewer and smaller product groups, compared to those whose main task is to buy manufacturer brand products. Hence, some buyers are responsible for only twenty or thirty items, while others have several hundred.

Representatives from the supplier companies contact the buyers, when they have a new product to offer. On a special offer form, prepared by KF, the supplier fills in various data about the product and market introduction plan. The buyer receives this form together with a few samples of the product and sometimes a few pamphlets and other written materials, after which he can start analysing the product's suitability for inclusion in the KF assortment. Of special importance are the sales figures for current products within the product group in question. Another very important type of input is the test results from KF's consumer panel. All new items must be blind-tested together with a few comparable products.

The final decisions are made by the assortment committee at KF headquarters, at monthly meetings lasting one or two days. The committee has 20 members: each of the 15 regional offices appoints one member, three are representatives for the regional warehouses and two come from the headquarters, including the vice-president in charge of food marketing, who holds the post of committee chairman. The rationale for the mixed composition of the committee - representing, as it does, a variety of professional and geographical backgrounds - is a desire to reflect the heterogeneity of the entire consumer cooperative enterprise. It should be noted, moreover, that the assortment committee also is responsible for the marketing plans (at the tactical level), though this work takes place at other sessions. All this means that all the tasks of the committee are of a tactical nature.

The buyers make personal, oral reports to the committee. After a discussion within the committee, decisions are reached immediately. There are often more than one hundred cases to be decided upon during one session of the committee, which means that a case decision generally takes five to ten minutes.

As mentioned above, the assortment committee's principal basis for decisions is the product fact sheets, supplied by the buyers. Nevertheless, the committee members also have several other sources of information in deciding cases. They test sample the products themselves, analyse the regional sales figures, etc. (See Section 3.5.) Taken together, all this information form a pattern, on which the committee bases its decisions.

We conclude this section with some characteristics of KF and its assortment building function - characteristics which are expected to be of importance for its choice criteria:

- The consumer cooperative movement is a very large conglomerate, whether measured in absolute terms or relatively in terms of its market share, and it is characterized by a very high degree of vertical integration.
- The integration means that the central level of the chain exerts strong influence on the assortments at all subsequent levels of the distribution channel.
- The total size of the assortment can therefore be kept comparatively limited. The firm has a generally restrictive attitude towards new products.
- The number of distributor brand products is large, produced both in the firm's own factories and by contract manufacturers.
- New products are subjected to very thorough examination, e.g., routine consumer panel tests.
- The entire assortment building function is performed in accordance with a highly routine and formalized pattern.
- The assortment building task is divided between an assortment committee, making the final decisions, and a number of buyers, analysing the cases and offering proposals to the committee.
- The assortment committee has many members, with quite varied backgrounds.
- There is a large number of buyers, most of whom are responsible for comparatively few products, and they not only make purchases from outside sources but are also product managers for distributor brand products.

3.3 The Consumer Cooperative Business Form

The enterprise being studied has a consumer cooperative business form. Hence, its ultimate goal may be said to be consumer interests and not profitability. (Nilsson 1983.) This notion requires some discussion, as by far the greater part of previous research seems to comprise studies of profit-oriented companies. Research on consumer cooperatives is apparently only to be found in Scandinavian studies, but none of these analyze the importance of specifically co-op characteristics for the assortment building function. (Gripsrud & Olsen 1975; Lindqvist 1976; Nilsson 1980.) The question, then, is to what extent current knowledge of reseller assortment decision criteria is valid also for consumer cooperatives. This knowledge is based on studies of profit-oriented companies, which are bound to have profitability as their ultimate criterion. (See Section 2.4.)

The fact that a consumer cooperative has consumer (member) interests as its ultimate goal does not preclude a profitability goal, subordinate to the ultimate goal. It is in the members' interest, and thus the enterprise's, that the organization acquires and utilizes its resources in the most efficient way. In the concept of consumer interest, there is always an economic dimension, which often might even be quite salient. Furthermore, the enterprise is generally competing with profit-oriented companies and working in a mainly profit-oriented environment, and this also influences its conception of its goals. (Nilsson 1983, p. 99-112.)

What role the profitability goal plays in the goal hierarchy of a consumer cooperative can vary considerably. There is a pronounced heterogeneity among consumer cooperatives with regard to cooperative identity. In some cases the profitability goal can have a very prominent position in the goal hierarchy, so that the enterprise becomes almost identical with profit-oriented companies, while in other instances the organization may exhibit a closer resemblance to the ideal type of consumer cooperative.

In the case of KF, the resemblance is closer to the profit-oriented type. Even though consumer interest may still be its primary goal, profitability has become very important. There are several indications of this:

- The enterprise is in tough competition with efficient companies pursuing a profitability goal.
- For the consumers, the economic dimension is immensely important, expressed, for example, in high price sensitivity.
- The enterprise has made heavy investments, among other things, in production facilities, which means that capital interests are expanding.
- Because of difficulties in financing business activities with equity capital, the organization has been forced to borrow heavily from external sources, and this further strengthens the influence of capital interests.

This leads us to the conclusion that there is sufficient warrant for analyzing KF's assortment decision criteria on the basis of all we already know about the criteria of profit-oriented enterprises. The organization must pursue a profitability goal in its assortment building, especially since this function is highly sensitive to market conditions and competition. Nevertheless, a certain caution is required. Cooperative ideology may very well be expressed in the manner of applying the profitability goal. The consumer cooperative characteristics could entail another way of looking at the criteria, and thus another way of weighting them, even though the total number of criteria is the same as in profit-oriented companies. (See Section 3.4.)

It should also be noted that the connections between decision criteria and goals at higher levels of the hierarchy are always unclear. (Kast 1974, pp. 160-161.) It is undeniable *that* the higher goals in some way determine the lower goals and, among these, decision criteria, but it is very difficult to explain *how*. As we do not know the subgoals located in the hierarchy, we can only speculate about the way in which the criteria are related to the ultimate goal - in our case, KF's consumer interest goal.

This supports our conclusion, that it is reasonable to use a very general list of criteria, such as the one presented in the preceding chapter. Nevertheless, their relative importance and interpretation remain to be seen, all the moreso, because it is a question of a consumer cooperative enterprise.

3.4 Assortment Decision Criteria

As mentioned in Section 3.1, KF's assortment decision criteria have been the subject of previous research. The period studied is identical with that of the present study. Its findings can be summarized as follows. (Nilsson 1980, pp. 133-135 and 166-199.) The criteria are arranged according to the list presented in Section 2.3.

A. Profitability and Sales
The dominant criteria for KF's assortment choices were found in the category "profitability and sales". The profitability goal is, however, seldom explicit in the deliberations. For the most part, it is discussed in terms of sales. It seems that the enterprise tries to maximize its sales, both in acceptance and deletion decisions. And the sales trend is normally more important than the absolute level of the sales volume.

B. Economic Conditions
Prices and other economic conditions are of very great importance in KF's assortment decisions. This is easily understood, considering the close connection with both profitability and the economic dimension of consumer interest. The great significance of the economic criteria is also expressed in the fact that the enterprise is very price sensitive in its choice of products and suppliers, and that it is a tough negotiation partner in relation to its suppliers. Furthermore, KF has a propensity to take over certain functions from its

suppliers, in order to obtain even lower prices - such as buying fixed quantities, transporting the goods itself and, in the extreme case, having the suppliers manufacture distributor brands.

C.   Assortment Considerations

For KF, it is very important to keep the size of the assortment strictly limited. This effort is shown in several ways:

- The principle of "one in, one out" is applied as often as possible.
- Assortment reviews are conducted regularly, i.e., critical analyses of various product groups result in appropriate deletions.
- There is a generally critical attitude towards new products, and relatively few new product offers are accepted. Old products enjoy a high priority in relation to new ones.
- Compared to what other studies report, KF makes very thorough and critical analyses of the new product offers. For example, all new products are routinely tested by a consumer panel.

There are, however, certain situations, where considerations of assortment limitation are set aside:

- When expanding sales figures for a product group are seen as a sign that the market is becoming large enough for more items in this product group.
- If a product is judged to be highly innovative.

KF has a large number of distributor brand items, and these enjoy high priority in all assortment decisions. Hence, the effect on distributor brands is always deliberated whenever manufacturer brand products are being reviewed for acceptance or deletion.

D.   Consumer Evaluations

To a remarkably high degree, KF's buyers consider the consumer to be a "rational decision maker." The price and the quality of the product are, thus, more important factors than its various psychological characteristics. The consumer panel test routine is also a sign of this "rational" consumer conception. All this is a manifestation of the consumer interest goal of the enterprise.

This does not mean, however, that all psychological factors are ruled out. Because of sales and profitability requirements, the buyers are also forced to consider the emotional buying motives of the consumer and the effects of supplier marketing on demand.

E. Marketing
The suppliers' marketing plans have, of course, a significant influence on KF's buying decisions, as marketing considerably influences consumer demand. Nevertheless, this introductory marketing is less appreciated and less important as a decision criterion in KF than it seems to be among resellers - as reported by other studies. The explanation is that KF for various reasons - cooperative ideology, large size and high degree of integration - wants to have full control of the assortment itself, and to remain independent of the suppliers.

A few further remarks on supplier marketing may be added:

- Continual marketing is a more important criterion than marketing in the introductory phase only.
- There are normally no evaluations of the various elements of the marketing plan, but only a statement that a campaign of a certain size and character is planned.
- The fact that a supplier is conducting a marketing campaign is sometimes interpreted as in indication of the supplier's confidence in his new product.

F. Supplier Characteristics
According to previous research, supplier reliability is one of the most important decision criteria, and this is intimately related to the suppliers' size, marketing skills, product program, administrative routines, etc. This holds true also for KF, though not to the same extent as reported in other studies. In KF, there is also a counteractive tendency to buy from moderate-sized and smaller suppliers, who do not dominate in the market. Firstly, it is easier to negotiate advantageous conditions (cf. B above); secondly, KF does not evaluate marketing skills as highly as other resellers seem to do (cf. E); thirdly, for KF, it is very important to avoid becoming dependent on strong suppliers (cf. I).

G. Competitive Considerations
Considerations regarding competing chains occur in KF's assortment decisions, though to a small extent. The influence of competitors is mainly indirect, namely, through consumer demand. Information on sales volume and prices of competitors is more important than information regarding the composition of competitor assortments.

H. Distributive Factors
It occurs only occasionally that assortment decisions are influenced by distributive factors. A supplier seldom presents a package which is unsuited for the store shelves, is too big for the smaller stores, is too bulky for the warehouses, etc.

I.   Tactical Considerations

As a rule, resellers seldom resort to conspicuously tactical measures against their suppliers. Such action requires, first of all, heavy concentration both at the production level and the distribution level. This is the case here. Secondly, it is normally only under unusual circumstances, that the reseller has a reason to act tactically.

On the basis of the preceding points, it should be clear that, compared to most other resellers, KF is more prone to act tactically. Its desire to have full control of its assortment; its pronounced ambition to negotiate very favorable economic conditions; its sceptical attitude towards the market's leading suppliers - this all fosters tactical action. Hence, it occasionally happens that KF suddenly and unexpectedly switches suppliers, divides its purchases between several suppliers, plays several suppliers off against each other, uses its own production plants as a means of pressure, etc.

J.   Salesman Presentation

At first glance, the supplier representatives generally have very limited importance for assortment decisions. Nevertheless, they seem to have some influence, though small, on the unconscious processes of the buyers. An attitude toward the salesman can be transferred to the product, and thus affect the decision.

3.5   Data Sources

The data set used in the present empirical study, is derived from the product fact sheets, presented in Section 3.2. (See Figure 3-3.) The product fact sheets, on which the buyers compile a variety of information of relevance for the decision cases, constitute the most important data basis for the assortment committee.

It should be noted, however, that the product fact sheets are not the only data basis for the assortment committee. The committee members also have information from five other sources:

- Most of the committee members are representatives of the various regions and regional warehouses, which means that they are especially attentive to regional sales trends. Hence, before the meeting, they study *the warehouses' sales statistics* for the products and product groups in question.
- Generally, the committee members get product samples from the suppliers, which they test either personally or through staff members. Thus, they have some *personal experience of the products.*
- It frequently happens that the committee members discuss the decision cases with a few *officials within their regional office or warehouse,* e.g., store managers or warehouse buyers.

- During *the buyer's personal presentation* before the committee, the buyer might provide additional oral or written information, such as results from consumer panel tests.
- The committee members have generally had a great deal of *business experience*, which has given them an in-depth knowledge of suppliers, marketing, distribution, etc. All this knowledge is, evidently, of importance for their decision making, even though it is seldom directly expressed at the meetings.

All these types of information do, of course, play a role in the decision making of the committee, and all contribute to the choice criteria. It is, however, impossible to specify in what way they exert their influence. Together, they form a pattern - a total information basis. Nevertheless, the product fact sheets clearly constitute the core of this information base. Product fact sheets are used in all decision cases; they give identical information to all committee members; they give information which is always of relevance for the decision cases; they give a rich variety of information; they present the information in a systematic and easily grasped manner; they are constructed solely to serve as the committee's information base.

Against this background we find it warranted to choose the product fact sheets as the sole data source of this study. Hence, we examine the relations between the information of the product fact sheets and the decision outcomes for a number of assortment decisions, well aware of the fact that the decision outcomes are also, to a certain extent, influenced by other types of information.

The buyers fill out one product fact sheet for each decision case, i.e., for each time a new product is considered for inclusion in the assortment or an old product is considered for deletion. In a single decision case, it may very well be that several new products are scrutinized simultaneously, or several old products, or both new and old products. Beside these "critical" products, i.e., products going into or disappearing from the assortment, the product fact sheet gives information about all the other products included in the product group in question, thus those competing with the "critical" products. Each product fact sheet, therefore, describes a given product group, characterizing its components according to a number of dimensions.

The product fact sheet is designed in such a way that the type of information given for new and old products is not entirely identical. This is readily understood; e.g., there are no sales statistics for new products, though perhaps a sales forecast; for old products date of delivery has no meaning; the number of regional warehouses carrying a product can be stated only for old products.

For the new products, the following facts are given on the product fact sheets:

- name of product,
- name of supplier,
- weight or volume per package,
- price per package (warehouse purchasing price),
- price per unit of weight or volume,
- delivery date,
- supplier marketing program, if any,
- sales forecast (only for accepted products),
- buyer suggestion of product's store classification (what size-type of store is the product suitable for?) (only for accepted products),
- consumer panel test results (can be omitted),
- decision outcome (accepted or rejected?).

For the old products, the following facts are given on the product fact sheets:

- name of product,
- name of supplier,
- weight or volume of package,
- price per package (warehouse's purchasing price),
- price per unit of weight or volume,
- sales volume during the last two years,
- store classification (what size-type of store is the product suitable for?)
- number of regional warehouses carrying the product,
- decision outcome (retained or deleted?).

There is no mention in previous studies of resellers using anything corresponding to KF's product fact sheets, i.e., special lists compiled by the buyers for the assortment committee. Several authors, however, do mention offer forms, which the resellers require the suppliers to fill in, when presenting their new products. (Borden 1968, p. 187; Grashof 1968, pp. 73-74 and p. 180; Heeler et al. 1973, p. 35; Arora 1975, p. 78 and p. 177; Hutt 1975, p. 23; Lindqvist 1976, p. 63 and p. 107; Bauer 1980, pp. 100-103; Nilsson 1980, pp. 45-48; Swinnen 1983, pp. 121-123.) Such offer forms are, of course, also used by KF, but there they are used to inform the buyer and serve as a basis for analysis and proposal. As the buyer makes up the product fact sheet, he obtains some of his information from the offer forms.

As no previous study mentions anything corresponding to the product fact sheets, this kind of data source has, of course, not been used before. One study, however, is based on data from offer forms. Heeler, Kearney and Mehaffey use data from offer forms for 67 new products, yielding 13 variables. (Heeler et al. 1973.)

Data collected from offer forms and from product fact sheets have some traits in common. Hence, what Heeler et al. wrote about their study, is also true for ours:

... the study reported here researched real behavior, and data were obtained from nonreactive archival records. No buyer knew in advance that his decisions were to be modeled. (Heeler et al. 1973, p. 35.)

In our opinion, product fact sheets have certain advantages compared to offer forms:

- The offer forms give information only about the product itself, while the product fact sheets present facts about all the other products in the product group as well as the product in question.
- The offer forms inform only about new products presented by suppliers, and hence, they can be used only in studies of acceptance decisions. Product fact sheets are compiled for all assortment changes, acceptance as well as deletion.
- The offer forms contain data originating from the supplier only, while the product fact sheets have data both from the supplier and the reseller.
- The offer forms give general information to the buyer. The product fact sheets are designed to give specific information to the assortment committee, as a basis for final decisions.

Almost all other studies are based on interviews with buyers and sometimes with other similar officials in the reseller companies. A common procedure is to first conduct a small number of unstructured interviews, and on the basis of these, the researcher designs a questionnaire for a larger number of buyers. (Doyle & Weinberg 1973; Sweitzer 1974; Montgomery 1975; Douglas 1980; Sauer 1982a; Swinnen 1982.) Other studies have used only unstructured interviews, though often in-depth interviews, of a case study character. (Grashof 1968; Johnson 1976; Lindqvist 1976.) Some researchers have used observation techniques of various kinds, normally combined with unstructured interviews with officials. (Hileman & Rosenstein 1961; Borden 1968; Berens 1969; Arora 1975; Nilsson 1980.)

One cannot say that one particular type of data source is the best in general. Each type has certain advantages and certain drawbacks, which should be taken into consideration. Therefore, the various data sources should be regarded as complementary rather than alternative. They provide different types of information, which can often be combined to further a better understanding of the subject matter. Hence, we consider it an asset, worth exploiting, that KF's assortment decision criteria have been researched before by one of the authors, and with a quite different method, namely participant observation - a method, furthermore, which in itself includes both observation and unstructured interviews. (See Sections 3.1 and 3.4.)

3.6   Data Collection

The study is based on product fact sheets presented at three assortment committee sessions in 1975. The data set consists of 54 decision cases, each dealing with one product group on the basis of one product fact sheet. The 54 product groups contain a total of 506 products, of which 87 are new and 419 are old ones. The product groups studied represent a wide spectrum of food items, for example, soup, cheese, mustard, pizza, marmalade, juice and drink mixes.

Of the new products, 39 (45%) were accepted, while 48 (55%) were rejected. The figures for the old products are 363 (87%) retentions and 56 (13%) deletions. It is seen that the number of deleted old products exceeds the number of accepted new products, which implies a reduction of the assortment size. This somewhat surprising outcome is due to the fact that, in the committee meetings studied, several comprehensive reviews took place, in which a large number of old products were weeded out of some product groups.

An interesting question is what factors determine which products and product groups are to be dealt with by the committee. Why are these particular product fact sheets with these particular 54 product groups forwarded to these three committee sessions, and not others? To answer that question, it is necessary to look at the new and old products separately. An in-depth analysis of the issue will not, however, be made, as this would also require studies of the assortment decision criteria of upper levels of the distribution channel, and we have stated in proposition h (Section 1.4) that this study is limited to the central wholesale level only.

By far the largest part of new product decisions (nearly 90 percent) are initiated by suppliers presenting new products to the enterprise. The buyers are obliged to convey all these new product offers to the assortment committee, even if they consider the product obviously unacceptable. The other new products are distributor brands, for which the buyers are also product managers. (However, as will be seen later in this section, it is necessary to exclude decisions on new distributor brands from the empirical analysis.)

All deletions of old products are decided by the committee - the buyers have no authority to delete products on their own. Deletions occur mainly in two situations. Firstly, when new products are considered for inclusion, the current products within the product group in question are always scrutinized. Secondly, the buyers make so-called assortment reviews of their various product groups once or twice a year. The aim of these is to "streamline" the composition of the product groups, and the result is normally that several products are deleted. Beside these two situations, it occasionally happens that products are deleted, because the suppliers cease to produce or import items.

The three committee meetings, from which the product fact sheets originate, were arbitrarily chosen and should show a random pattern. The meetings took place in different seasons within a seven month period. There is nothing to support a presumption that the data might systematically deviate from the organization's total assortment decisions in this period. There is, however, no possibility of checking the representativeness of the data, as there are no corresponding data from other assortment decisions in the enterprise.

Similarly, it is impossible to tell to what extent the data are representative for KF's assortment decisions in other years, earlier and later, or to say anything about the representativeness in relation to the assortment decisions of other resellers. The issue of representativeness is, however, only of minor interest, as it is evident that assortment decision criteria are closely related to the specific conditions of a given reseller, that these conditions change over time, and that different resellers work under widely divergent conditions. (See the discussion about contingency in Section 1.6 and about incompatibilities in the previous research in Section 2.3.)

How the product groups are defined, i.e., which products are considered as belonging to the same product group, is decided by the buying departments. Their criterion is that a product group should consist of all those products which the consumer is likely to consider as alternative choices, hence products considered as substitutes for each other in reseller assortment decisions. Consequently, a product group consists of a number of directly competing products. The size of the product groups varies considerably, from one til 29 products. In our analyses, we use the same product groups as the firm does.

In order to obtain a basis for comparisons, we divide the total data set into various decision categories, each of which can be analyzed separately. First of all, it is necessary to distinguish between two main categories, viz., decisions regarding new products to be accepted or rejected, and decisions regarding old products to be retained or deleted. The reason for this is evident: these two types of decisions are made on the basis of quite different types of information. (See Sections 1.3 and 3.5.)

The way in which these two main categories are further divided into subcategories depends on the partial homogeneities of the data set. Each subcategory must contain constituent decisions which are as similar as possible to each other and as dissimilar as possible to other subcategories. This is determined on theoretical grounds and on the basis of expectations derived from previous research as well as statistical considerations. The latter are described in Section 4.4. The resulting grouping of the data set into decision categories is shown in Figure 3-4.

Thus, we distinguish between decisions concerning manufacturer brand products and distributor brand products. Previous research - in general as well as the previous study of KF - indicates clearly that the origin of the products is a crucial factor in the assortment decisions. The findings from our statistical computations also confirm this.

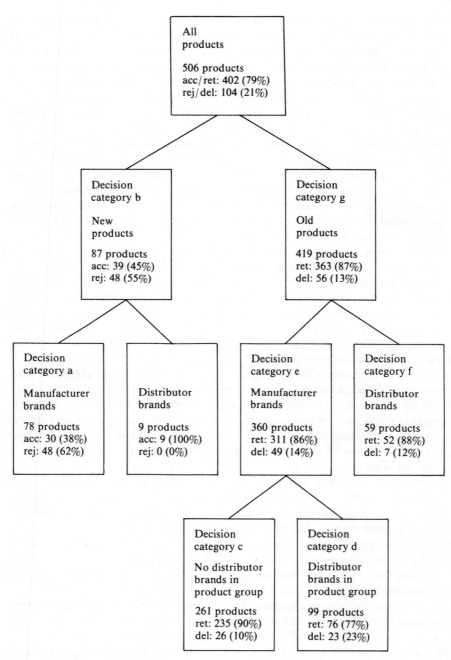

Figure 3-4: Decision Categories in the Data Set

When this classification is combined with the former one, four decision categories appear. One of these, viz., old manufacturer brand products, contains a large and very heterogeneous group of decisions. It is, therefore, both possible and desirable to further subdivide this category. Again on the basis of both statistical considerations and experience from previous research, the issue of distributor versus manufacturer brands turns out to be crucial. Thus, this decision category is further divided into two less heterogeneous subcategories - one where there are no distributor brands in the product groups and another where the product groups contain at least one distributor brand product.

Figure 3-4 shows, first of all, that the total set of 506 products is not considered as a decision category to be analyzed as a whole. It is meaningless to aggregate decisions concerning new and old products, because, as mentioned above, they are extremely dissimilar. Likewise, it is meaningless to aggregate either new and old distributor brand products or new and old manufacturer brand products.

Secondly, Figure 3-4 shows that the decision category regarding new distributor brand products is omitted. The reason for this is that the products in this category are always accepted due to some specific decision routines within the committee: the buyers include only new products which have already been accepted by the committee or by a subcommittee during the product development process. This decision category also happens to be too small to be analyzed meaningfully - only nine products.

From what has been said above, it is seen that we aggregate decisions made by different decision makers into common decision categories. This could be problematic, as the decision makers might have applied somewhat different criteria or followed somewhat different decision rules. (See Section 4.6) To the extent that these differences lead to heterogeneity in the data set, the findings become uncertain. (Bauer 1980, pp. 332-336.)

In our study, however, this problem proves to be of less significance than in most other studies on reseller decision criteria. First of all, it is the assortment committee which makes the final and formal decisions, and the composition of the committee did not change during the time period studied. So, all the decisions were made by the same group of individuals. Secondly, it is true that the committee tends to accept the proposals of the buyers, but there are also many exceptions to this. As it is quite embarrassing for the buyer to have his proposal turned down by the committee, he tries to learn and adapt to the norms of the committee, and ultimately, he internalizes these norms. This all means that the differences between the buyers and the committee members and between the various buyers are not very great.

As explained in Section 1.3, it is always rational for a reseller to take a conservative attitude to assortment decision making, implying that in cases of uncertainty, old products should be retained and new products should be rejected. The data in Figure 3-4 indicate that this principle is clearly manifested in KF. For example, nearly two thirds of the new products in category a are rejected, and nine tenths of the old products in category c are retained. Actually, one would expect this conservative attitude to be quite pronounced in KF, because its high degree of vertical integration means that potential losses caused by faulty deletion and acceptance decisions are aggravated. This supposition is also confirmed by the fact that KF's largest competitor, which is considerably less integrated, accepts about 70 percent of all the suppliers' new offers. (Nilsson 1980, p. 28.)

3.7   Variables

The present study differs from previous research by focusing on the interdependence between different product decisions. If, for example, a new product is accepted and, on the same occasion, an old product is deleted from the same product group, we consider it incorrect to treat these two decisions as independent of each other. The situation is the same if two or more new products are accepted simultaneously, of if two or more old products are deleted simultaneously. (Cf. Section 2.2.)

Hence, we consider the assortment decision to consist of several concurrent and *conjoined decisions* determining a product group's overall composition in terms of a specific number of new and old products. Rather than study each product decision in isolation, we consider it more useful to conceive the decision as affecting the total composition of the assortment in a given product group.

The compound decision denotes that the assortment committee works with two sets of products: 1) all the old products, i.e., those currently in the assortment, and 2) all the new products, i.e., those not in the assortment. From these two sets, the committee chooses a certain number to form a new and differently composed product group. All the products, new and old, are in competition with one another. (See Section 1.3 and Figure 1-1.)

Hence, the focus of the study is shifted from single product decisions to the composition of and changes in the whole product group. This necessarily presupposes that the assortment committee arranges the assortment of one product group independently of the composition of other product groups. Such an assumption seems reasonable. At the committee meetings, each product group is treated separately.

In order to describe the composition of a product group, specific product data must be used. Some data are characteristics of the products, seen separately. Examples of such *product specific variables* are supplier identity, the number of regional warehouses carrying the product and introductory marketing campaigns.

Other data are estimates of the products' values in relation to other products in the product group. Examples of such *product related variables* are the relative price of the product, its share of the total sales volume and the relative size of its package.

It is, however, also necessary to grasp the total product group, in order to take into account the interdependence between the various products. This can be done by introducing new variables, which serve to link decisions concerning different products within the product group. Examples of such *product group variables* are the size of the product group, changes in product group size and occurrence of distributor brands in the product group.

As our data source is the distributor's product fact sheets, we are not free to choose any variable among the criteria presented in Sections 2.3 and 2.4. We are limited to criteria which we can deduce from the product fact sheets. Hence, we have compiled the following list of 15 variables: one response variable and 14 potential criteria.

RESPONSE = Decision outcome: (1) a new product is accepted or an old one retained, (2) a new product is rejected or an old one deleted.

GRPSALE = Sales trend of the product group, i.e., the preceding year's sales volume as a percentage of the previous year's (no matter whether the number of products is larger or smaller).

GRPSIZE = Size of the product group, i.e., the number of products in the product group before the decision.

GRADSIZE = Gradual change in the size of the product group, subsequent to the decision, but excluding the product under consideration.

DISTRIB = Existence of distributor brands in the product group: (1) at least one distributor brand product, apart from the product under consideration, (0) otherwise.

PRICE = Relative price per weight or volume, i.e., the price of one weight or volume unit of the product as a percentage of the corresponding price of the closest competing product.

SIZE = Package size, i.e., the product's consumer package size as a percentage of the size of the most sold product in the product group.

NEWNESS = Evaluation of the product's degree of newness, based on its functions, design, features, etc.: (1) the product is completely unique, (2) different, (3) largely identical with current products. (Two dummy variables are defined for levels 1 and 2.)

SHARE = Share of the product group's sales volume, i.e., the product's sales volume the preceding year as a percentage of the sales volume of the total product group.

MARKLEAD = Supplier identity, though only in cases of manufacturer brands: (1) the supplier is a market leader, (0) otherwise.

OWNPROD = Product identity: (1) the supplier is the distributor, i.e., a distributor brand, (0) otherwise, i.e., a manufacturer brand.

CAMPAIGN = Supplier introductory marketing campaign: (1) the supplier is planning an advertising and sales promotion campaign to support the market introduction of the product, (0) otherwise.

PRODSALE = Sales trend of the product, i.e., the product's sales volume the preceding year as a percentage of its sales during the previous year.

REGHOUSE = Number of regional warehouses carrying the product.

STORE = Store size (measured in annual gross revenue), i.e., the smallest stores for which the assortment committee recommends the product.

This list of variables requires some explanation and comment:

- On the product fact sheets, sales volume is most often expressed by the number of package units, only occasionally in units of weight or volume, and never in monetary units. The calculations of values of the variables GRPSALE, SHARE and PRODSALE are all based on the figures of the product fact sheets. This principle might be debated in the case of the first two variables, as in some product groups there are great differences in package sizes. Nevertheless, we consider it reasonable, since the buying committee uses the number of units in its deliberations.
- It is seen that in the variable PRICE, the product is related to the closest competing product. Conceivably, the cheapest product or the most sold product might also serve as a point of reference, but, in our opinion, neither of these alternatives would make as much sense. The cheapest product generally has an extremely large package, or it is of very low quality. Similarly, the most sold product is often relatively cheap, and its characteristics could differ from those of the product in question. As our purpose is to simulate the decision process of the assortment committee, we

prefer to relate the product under consideration to products which, because of taste, package size, functions, etc., are expected to be close substitutes in the minds of the decision makers.

- Having said this, it should be clear that there is a subjective element in the coding of the variable PRICE. There is no objective way to assess which products are the closest competing. The choice is our own, based on both general and more detailed knowledge of the grocery industry. Our criterion for the closest competing product is what the assortment committee would supposedly choose, if the product under consideration did not exist. Hence, the competing product is often somewhat cheaper.

- The relative price of the product could alternatively be expressed as price per package. Such a price variable is, however, excluded for two reasons. Firstly, computations show that there is a high correlation between a price variable, so defined, and the definition we have chosen for PRICE, i.e., price per weight or volume unit, so, only one of them should be used. Secondly, we consider the latter formulation to reflect the deliberations of the assortment committee more accurately.

- In operationalizing the variable SIZE, it is not the product's relation to any other specific product, which is of interest, but the product's relation to all the products of the product group, i.e., whether it is smaller or larger than others. This is the reason why the package size of the most sold product is used as the term of reference for all products.

- The suppliers' names are mentioned on the product fact sheets, but there is no evaluation of them. The evaluations are in the minds of the decision makers. As supplier identity, according to previous studies both of KF and generally, can be an important criterion, we consider it highly desirable to include this variable. We had, however, to make a classification of our own, and we have chosen the simple but crucial question of whether the supplier is a market leader or not, i.e., the variable MARKLEAD. Based on our knowledge of the grocery industry, we identify the dominant supplier in each product group as a market leader. It is evident that there is a subjective element in these codings, but, in our opinion, it is unlikely that there are any significantly incorrect identifications.

- The classification of the variable NEWNESS is likewise based on our own subjective evaluations of the new products. The subjective element, and hence the degree of uncertainty, is probably appreciable, but since findings from other studies indicate that this criterion might be of great importance, we have decided to include it.

- KF has a test routine for new products. There is a consumer panel, which tastes samples of the new products and compares them with a few of the competing old products. On the product fact sheets there is room to enter the results of these tests. According to the previous study of KF, the test results constitute a very important decision criterion, and therefore, we

Applicability of criteria Charac- teristics of criteria	Applicable for both new and old product decisions	Applicable only for new product decisions	Applicable only for old product decisions	Number of variables
Product group variables	a) GRPSALE b) GRPSIZE c) GRADSIZE d) DISTRIB	-	-	4
Product related variables	e) PRICE f) SIZE	g) NEWNESS	h) SHARE	4
Product specific variables	i) MARKLEAD j) OWNPROD	k) CAMPAIGN	l) PRODSALE m) REGHOUSE n) STORE	6
Number of variables	8	2	4	14

Figure 3-5: Characteristics of the Explanatory Variables (Criteria)

consider it highly desirable that this variable is included. This proved, however, to be impossible, as the buyers too often failed to note the test results on the product fact sheets when they recommended the rejection of a new product. Hence, incompleteness of data forced us to omit this variable.

- Of the 14 criteria mentioned above, not all are applicable to both new and old product decisions. The product group variables, i.e., GRPSALE, GRPSIZE, GRADSIZE and DISTRIB, can of course be used for both types of decisions. The same holds true for PRICE, SIZE, OWNPROD and MARKLEAD. For the other product related and product specific variables, the situation varies. NEWNESS and CAMPAIGN are characteristics of new products only. The variables SHARE, PRODSALE, REGHOUSE and STORE all presuppose that the products are already in the assortment. As for STORE, it must be noted that the assortment committee assigns a store class to new items only if they are accepted, but there is no corresponding data for the rejections. Consequently, this variable cannot be used for new products. Figure 3-5 summarizes this discussion in a schematic form.

A crucial question is how well the 14 explanatory variables correspond to the actual decision criteria applied by the assortment committee. On the one hand, the list of variables has certain limitations:

- The product fact sheets may be the main decision basis for the assortment committee, but it is not the only one. There are others, which are not included in the study: the regional sales statistics, personal impressions from product samples, some staff members' views of the products, buyer presentations and the committee members' background information and experience. (See Section 3.5.)
- It has not been possible to use all the information contained in the product fact sheets. We regret, in particular, that we had to omit the panel test results. Likewise, delivery dates and the number of consumer packages per store package had to be given up because of inadequate data.
- It cannot be ruled out, that some of the operationalizations of the variables, presented above, fail to fully reflect the perceptions of the decision makers. It should be remembered that what is of ultimate importance for decision making is not the data in themselves - prices, sales volumes, package sizes, etc. - but the decision maker's conception of these data; and this is very difficult to operationalize.

On the other hand, judging from what we already know in general about assortment decision criteria as well as from the findings of the previous study of KF, the list includes numerous variables which may be expected to prove important. Hence, in Figure 3-6, our variables are coupled with the general classification of criteria, presented in Section 2.3. The proviso should be added that our study deals with both acceptance and deletion decisions, while nearly all previous research has concentrated on acceptance, and the earlier study of KF did not distinguish stringently between the two decision types.

Figure 3-6 provides a basis for the following observations:

- All the main classes of criteria reported to be of central importance in previous research (A,B,C,D,E and F) are represented by at least one variable.
- Likewise, our variables belong predominantly to those classes which other researchers point out as the most important, viz., A3 Sales potential, C2 Relations to other products, E1 Introductory marketing campaign and F2 Supplier reputation and reliability.
- On the negative side, the important main class, B Economic conditions, is inadequately covered by our variables. The reason for this is that gross margins, discounts and support to cooperative advertising is seldom explicitly discussed during the decision-making process. This information

Criteria classes	Number of times in earlier studies	Importance according to Nilsson 1980	Variable
A. **Profitability and sales**			
A1 Overall profitability	12	v.i.	
A2 Rate of turnover	7	i.	REGHOUSE
A3 Sales potential	31	v.i.	PRODSALE; SHARE
B. **Economic conditions**			
B1 Supplier's price	6	v.i.	PRICE
B2 Gross margin	14	i.	-
B3 Allowances and rebates	17	i.	-
B4 Support to cooperative advertising	13	i.	-
B5 Credit terms	7		-
B6 Other economic conditions	18		-
C. **Assortment considerations**			
C1 Existence of distributor brands	3	v.i.	DISTRIB
C2 Relation to other products	18	v.i.	GRPSALE; GRPSIZE GRADSIZE; SHARE; NEWNESS
D. **Consumer evaluation**			
D1 Overall consumer value	20	v.i.	-
D2 Retail price	11	v.i.	PRICE
D3 Product's physical characteristics	18	v.i.	-
D4 Product's psychological characteristics	13	i.	NEWNESS
D5 Packaging	13		SIZE

E.	Supplier marketing				
	E1 Introductory				
	marketing campaign	34	i.	CAMPAIGN.	
	E2 Continuous				
	marketing	17	v.i.	-	
F.	Supplier characteristics				
	F1 Supplier				
	representative	5		-	
	F2 Reputation and				
	reliability	30	i.	MARKLEAD; OWNPROD	
	F3 Sales force				
	organization	5		-	
	F4 Services and				
	functions	33	i.	-	
	F5 Other characteristics	6		-	
G.	Competitive				
	considerations	13		-	
H.	Distributive factors				
	H1 Transportation				
	adaptation	4		-	
	H2 Store adaptation	11		(SIZE); STORE	
I.	Tactical considerations	3	i.	-	
J.	Salesman presentation	7		-	

Figure 3-6: The Variables of the Study, Related to the General Classification of Criteria. (i. = important; v.i. = very important.)

is stored in the heads of the decision makers, but not stated on the product fact sheets.
- According to previous research, criterion F4, Supplier's services and functions, is quite important. The reason why there is nothing corresponding to this on the product fact sheet is probably that the committee members already have a knowledge of most suppliers' business policies or that the buyers mention these facts in their oral presentations. It is, of course, unfortunate that there is no variable in this criterion class, but there might be some overlap between classes F2 and F4, so the variable MARKLEAD may to some extent also represent class F4.

- Half of the criteria which the previous study of KF's assortment building noted as important (i. in Figure 3-6) are represented by our variables. The proportion is the same with regard to the variables noted as very important (v.i. in Figure 3-6) in that study.

The deficiencies to which we have drawn attention preclude a mapping of KF's decision criteria that is satisfactory in every respect. But, on balance, we are satisfied that the variables we have defined represent a range of criteria that is numerous and varied enough to promise a rich yield of interesting results.

4 STATISTICAL ANALYSES

4.1 Outline of the Chapter

The purpose of this chapter is to present and evaluate the logit model and the logistic regression analysis, which are the statistical model and analysis used in this study. The basis for choosing the statistical model is the research problem and quality of data.

Data is described in Section 4.2. The fundamentals of the logit model are given in Section 4.3, while a more elaborate technical treatment is found in Appendix A.

The problem of selection between different logit models (selecting predictor variables) is discussed on the basis of both theoretical and statistical arguments in Section 4.4. In Section 4.5 a special goodness of fit measure suited to statistical models and analyses with a binary response variable is introduced. An evaluation of the statistical method chosen and a comparison with other possible methods is found in Section 4.6.

4.2 Data Structure and Missing Values

As mentioned in Section 3.6, the total data set of 506 product decisions is divided into various groups. Seven decision categories are defined, including both main categories and subcategories. Then the data set within each of these categories can be represented by a matrix

$$
\begin{bmatrix}
y_1 & x_{11} & \cdots & x_{p1} \\
y_2 & x_{12} & \cdots & x_{p2} \\
\cdot & & & \\
\cdot & & & \\
\cdot & & & \\
y_n & x_{1n} & \cdots & x_{pn}
\end{bmatrix}
$$

where

n	is the number of product decisions (observations),
p	is the number of decision criteria (predictor variables),
y_j	is the jth value of the decision outcome (response variable) Y: y_j = 1 (acceptance/ retention) or y_j = 0 (rejection/deletion),
x_{ij}	is the jth value of the decision criterion (predictor variable) X_i (i=1,2,...,p).

Depending on which decision category it concerns, the value of n varies from 59 to 419 (see Figure 3-4) and the value of p varies from 10 to 12 (see Figure 3-5).

In the data matrix there turns out to be a certain number of missing values, though very skewly distributed over the variables. They also occur twice as frequently among the old products as among the new. Of the 419 old products, 86 (21%) have missing values on at least one variable, while the corresponding figure for the 87 new products is 10 (11%).

The occurrence of missing values has largely different reasons in these two product decision categories:

- By far the greatest part of the missing values among the *old products* is due to the fact that there are many recently introduced products, i.e., products which have been in the assortment for such a short period that there are no complete sales figures for them. To compute a PRODSALE value (15% missing), the product must have been sold for at least 15 months. If a product has been for sale only a few months, there are no sales figures at all presented, so it is not possible to compute a value for SHARE (5% missing). Likewise, the REGHOUSE value is lost (9% missing), if the regional warehouses have not yet had time to have the product stocked. In certain product groups, predominantly very small ones, there may be so many recently introduced products that the GRPSALE value loses any significance (4% missing).
- With regard to the *new products*, it happens occasionally that a supplier introduces a product which is so different that there are no similar products in the assortment. Hence, the buyer has to consider it as a product group of its own, reporting it on a separate product fact sheet. It is then not possible to calculate certain of the product group and product related variables, which explains why there are a few missing values for GRPSALE, PRICE and SIZE, (7, 6 and 3, respectively).

4.3 The Logit Model

The statistical analysis chosen is logistic regression analysis, which is based on the logit probability model. A description of the logit model and its relation to the linear probability model, which is the theoretical basis of the ordinary linear regression analysis, is given in Appendix A.

The fundamental assumption of the logit model is the following. For a given value of the predictor variables x_1, x_2,..., x_p, the probability of the response variable Y to be 1 is given by the formula

$$P = \frac{1}{1+e^{-\beta_0 - \beta_1 x_1 - \beta_2 x_2 - .. - \beta_p x_p}} \qquad (4.1)$$

where $ß_0$ is the constant term and $ß_1$, $ß_2$, ..., $ß_p$ the regression coefficients. When presenting the estimation results, it is convenient to apply an alternative formulation of equation (4.1), that is

$$\text{Logit } P = \frac{P}{1-P} = \beta_0 + \beta_1 x_1 + \beta_2 x_2 + .. + \beta_p x_p \qquad (4.2)$$

In the next chapter, where the findings are presented, the estimated coefficients $ß_0$, $ß_1$, $ß_2$, ..., $ß_p$ and their standard errors are found for each of the presented logit models. As the logit transformation is strictly increasing, a positive (negative) regression coefficient causes an increase (a decrease) in the probability P.

To perform the statistical calculations we use the computer package BMDP Statistical Software. (Engelman 1981.)

4.4 Selection of Explanatory Variables

After the choice of statistical model and computer program, the problem of selecting explanatory variables among the candidates of possible predictor variables presents itself. For each of the two main decision categories, new and old products, the primary purpose is to find a logit model that, according to some prior expectations, statistical tests and goodness of fit measures, gives the most plausible explanation of data.

There will probably be found heterogeneity within the two decision categories, so in searching for more specific and detailed explanations, it is necessary to split the two categories into more homogeneous subcategories. This creation of decision subcategories takes place according to prior considerations and must, of course, obey some minimum restrictions concerning the number of observations in the subcategories. (Cf. Section 3.6.)

The optimal strategy for searching out the best logit model in each of the decision categories depends on which of the possible predictor variables are given high priority, and which are given low priority by the researcher. In the primary stage of the analysis, we therefore perform a stepwise logistic regression analysis on all possible predictor variables. Then we exclude those predictor variables with minimum or low priority, if the variables are not supported by data.

The explanatory variables in the final logit model can be characterized as

1. variables with high or low priority, if their coefficients are strongly significant or
2. variables with high priority, if their coefficients are moderately significant.

With this procedure for selecting the explanatory variables, all candidates are given a fair chance of being members of the final logit equation.

There is always a risk that some of the predictor variables may be so highly correlated, that the estimation and the interpretation of the coefficients create difficulties. In order to control for such a multicollinearity, we carry out factor analysis on the battery of predictor variables, but no such serious problems are detected, and in the final logit models no extreme correlations of the coefficients are found.

4.5 Goodness of Fit Measures

In linear regression analysis, the most common goodness of fit measure is the coefficient of determination R^2. It measures the proportion of the variation of the response variable (decision outcome) Y explained by the explanatory variables (decision criteria). When the response variable is dichotomous, however, R^2 is a poor goodness of fit measure, because R^2 is not likely to give values close to 1, even if the model fits well.

Hence, instead of R^2 we use the proportion of correct classifications PCC computed from the so-called classification table. This table is a cross tabulation of the actual decision outcomes y = 0 and y = 1 with the corresponding predicted decision outcomes $\hat{y}$ = 0 and $\hat{y}$ = 1 (rejection/deletion as opposed to acceptance/retention). The prediction of a product decision to be $\hat{y}$ = 0 or $\hat{y}$ = 1 is determined by defining a critical value for the estimated probability $\hat{P}_j = \hat{P}(Y_j = 1)$ in the following way: $\hat{y}_j = 1$, if $\hat{P}_j \geqslant 1/2$ and $\hat{y}_j = 0$, if $\hat{P}_j \leqslant 1/2$.

If the number of observations (product decisions) in the decision group is n, and n_0 and n_1 the number of cases, where y is 0 and 1, respectively, then the classification table can be described as follows:

	Number of cases		
Actual decision outcome	Predicted decision outcome		
	$\hat{y} = 1$	$\hat{y} = 0$	Total
y = 1	n_{11}	n_{10}	$n_{1+} = n_1$
y = 0	n_{01}	n_{00}	$n_{0+} = n_0$
Total	n_{+1}	n_{+0}	n

By dividing the table with the total number of observations and introducing $P_{ij} = n_{ij}/n$, we obtain

	Proportion of cases		
Actual decision outcome	Predicted decision outcome $\hat{y} = 1$	$\hat{y} = 0$	Total
$y = 1$	P_{11}	P_{10}	$P_{1+} = P_1$
$y = 0$	P_{01}	P_{00}	$P_{0+} = P_0$
Total	P_{+1}	P_{+0}	1

The proportion of correct classifications consists of correctly predicted acceptances/retentions (P_{11}) and correctly predicted rejections/deletions (P_{00}). Hence, the proportion of correct classifications by using the estimated model is the sum of these two, that is, PCC = $P_{11}+P_{00}$.

This number may be compared with the maximum chance criterion C_{max} = $\max(P_1,P_0)$. This number can be interpreted as the proportion of correct classifications, if the explanatory variables are not used in the prediction. Without knowledge of any explanatory variable, the best estimate would be to presuppose all products to be accepted/retained if $P_1 \geqslant 1/2$, or all products to be rejected/deleted if $P_0 \leqslant 1/2$. This decision procedure will result in a PCC equal to C_{max}. Consequently the difference $(P_{11} + P_{00})$ -C_{max} is the improvement of the PCC by introducing the explanatory variables in the decision model.

When, however, the prior distribution is skew, that is, $P_1 \neq P_0$, then the difference $(P_{11} + P_{00})$ - C_{max} is an all too pessimistic criterion for the predictor variables' ability to discriminate between the two decision outcomes y = 1 and y = 0. This is because C_{max} will overestimate the PCC when there are no predictor variables at hand. (Morrison 1969.)

Now suppose $P_1 \ll P_0$, and we want to identify the decision outcomes y = 1. Then obviously, it won't do to classify all outcomes as y = 0, that is to say, $\hat{y} = 0$. Looking at the classification table, we now ask: What is the PCC when the predicted and the actual decision outcomes are independent events, that is, when the predictor variables have no explanatory/discriminating power? The result is $P_{+1} \cdot P_1 + P_{+0} \cdot P_0$, which is called Morrison's modified proportion chance criterion, MC_{pro}. If the predicted and the actual (prior) distributions are identical, that is, $P_{+1} = P_1$ and $P_{+0} = P_0$, we get the (unmodified) Morrison's $C_{pro} = P_1^2 + P_0^2$. It follows from this discussion that the evaluation of the models should be based on the comparison of the two criteria: PCC =$P_{11}+P_{00}$ and $MC_{pro} = P_{+1} \cdot P_1 + P_{+0} \cdot P_0$.

As a final comment concerning the goodness of fit measures based on the classification table, it should be noted that they suffer from an upward bias due to classifying the same products as are used to calculate the logistic regression equation. We do not, however, find it necessary to solve this problem by using the "jackknife method."

Also the converged value of the log likelihood function (defined in formula (A.12) in Appendix A) is used as a goodness of fit measure in the selection process. Nevertheless, only the proportion of correct classifications will be presented (in Section 5.2), because the log likelihood function in our study shows consistency with PCC in ranking the different logit models (and therefore is superfluous), and because the PCC can be given a more intuitive and straightforward interpretation.

4.6   Discussion

Both the linear probability model and the logit model belong, in principle, to the class of *compensatory* models or decision rules. A compensatory model incorporates trade-offs between the criteria or predictor variables of the model, which means that an impairment in the value of one predictor variable (attribute) can be compensated by an improvement in another predictor variable.

Contrary to this type of decision rules are the *non-compensatory* models. These presuppose that an unsatisfactory value in one attribute cannot be compensated by satisfactory values in other respects. So, only alternatives which meet certain minimum requirements are accepted. Among the non-compensatory models, there are several types - conjunctive, disjunctive, lexicographic and various variants and combinations.

The *conjunctive* model implies that the decision maker accepts/retains the product, if it fulfills thresholds on a number of key criteria. If any criterion is deficient, the product is rejected/deleted.

In a *disjunctive* model only one attribute stands out as a selection criterion. The alternative which ranks highest on this attribute is the one preferred.

A *lexicographic* model assumes that all attributes are used, but in a stepwise manner. Products are evaluated on the most important criterion first. Then, if there are ties (two products are ranked equally according to this criterion), a second attribute is used, and so forth.

It is readily understood that the outcome of a choice situation could vary considerably, depending on which of these decision rules is applied. Hence, in attempts to attain theoretical understanding of actual decision making, it is important that a decision rule is chosen and designed in such a way that it corresponds to the decision makers' type of deliberations.

The question of which decision rule best represents real-life reseller assortment decisions is a debated issue. The decision rules are theoretical constructs, so it is not likely that any of them could be a perfect reflection of reality. Rather, actual decision making is bound to be characterized by a combination of two or more of these abstract models. (See Bauer 1980, p. 340 and Swinnen 1983, Chap. 4, Sect III.)

... standard levels of attributes, interaction and compensatory effects may characterize the new product decisions. Consequently, neither the compensatory, nor the conjunctive, disjunctive or lexicographic order model, is able to fully capture the choice process.

Therefore, some extensions of these models are needed, that allow for compensatory and non-compensatory (i.e., "hybrid") decision rules. The inclusion of factors that link two or more criteria is one such possibility. Another illustration of the "hybrid" model is the gatekeeper analysis of Montgomery (1975) ... (Swinnen 1983, p. 133-134.)

This notwithstanding, we use the logit model, though it is a compensatory model. Firstly, we have sought to overcome the deficiencies that the model might have, by including only subsets of all the possible predictor variables in the final estimated logit models for the different decision categories. (See Section 4.4.) As will be seen in Chapter 5, the number of predictor variables in the logit models ranges from two to five, i.e., we allow for compensation only between these few variables. This principle means that non-compensatory elements are added to the logit model actually used, so that this acquires a certain "hybrid" character.

Secondly, Heeler, Kearney and Mehaffey (1973) made a comparison between the predictory ability of compensatory, disjunctive and conjunctive models in reseller assortment decisions. They found that the compensatory model turned out to be by far the best one.

Finally, it seems reasonable that among the pure decision rules, the compensatory model dominates in decision making regarding reseller assortment building. Compensatory reasoning is bound to occur more or less in all assortment decision cases.

... the following general thesis seems plausible: the more simple the decision situation, i.e., the fewer objects, evaluative criteria and levels of these criteria, the more likely it is that the individual has a reserve of cognitive capacity to manage a compensatory evaluation strategy (which represents the most frequently used of all strategies). As the new product decision can be characterized as comparatively uncomplicated, a compensatory application of the decision criteria is to be expected. (Bauer 1980, p. 319. Our translation.)

The comparison between the linear probability model and the logit model in Appendix A gives the arguments for choosing logistic regression instead of linear regression or linear discriminant analysis. Heeler, Kearney and Mehaffey (1973) used the discriminant analysis. Our data is more likely to fulfill the logit model than the linear probability model and therefore linear regression and discriminant analysis can be rejected.

The so-called "gatekeeper" analysis (Montgomery 1975) and the two other distribution-free methods DISFRE and DISOUT (Swinnen 1983) can be rejected for the following reasons: the relatively large number of observations and the measurement scales of the predictor variables (nominal and ratio) make it possible to use very efficient statistical estimation and testing procedures. The logistic regression analysis includes both maximum likelihood estimation and likelihood ratio testing procedures as well. In the search for the best model we think that the possibility of statistical testing (both goodness of fit of the model as well as testing the effect of the different criteria on the response variable) should be given the highest priority, and this is not the case, if we use the "gatekeeper," DISFRE or DISOUT method.

Instead of logit analysis, we could have used probit analysis. Experience shows, however, that we would obtain almost the same estimation results and conclusions, but at higher computer costs.

5 FINDINGS

5.1 Outline of the Chapter

As the findings of the study concern various decision criteria in various decision categories, there are two modes of structuring the presentation of the results. Since they produce different kinds of insights, both of them are utilized in this chapter. Section 5.2 thus gives an account of each of the seven decision categories, while Section 5.3 presents each of the fourteen potentially valid decision criteria. Finally, Section 5.4 discusses the findings of the study on a more general, aggregate level.

In Section 5.2, the logit model of each decision category is presented and evaluated. There are also very short and general discussions of the criteria

Decision categories (Section 5.2)	Acceptance/rejection of new products		Retention/deletion of old products				
	a) Manufacturer brands	b) Both manufacturer and distributor brands	Manufacturer brands			f) Distributor brands	g) Both manufacturer and distributor brands
Decision criteria (Section 5.3)			c) Product groups without distributor brands	d) Product groups with distributor brands	e) All product groups		
a. GRPSALE	.....	.....	.....	.....	.....	.....	.....
b. GRPSIZE	.....	.....	.....	0.157	0.175	.....	0.105
c. GRADSIZE	.....	.....	.....	0.459	0.279	.....	0.189
d. DISTRIB	-1.40	.....	-	-	-0.683	.....	-0.691
e. PRICE	-0.0157	-0.0214	.....	.....	.....	.....	.....
f. SIZE	.....	.....	.....	.....	.....	.....	.....
g. NEWNESS	.....	.....	-	-	-	-	-
h. SHARE	-	-	.....	.....	.....	.....	.....
i. MARKLEAD	.....	.....	-1.45	-1.26	.....	-	.....
j. OWNPROD	.....	.....	-	-	-	-	.....
k. CAMPAIGN	1.41	0.996	-	-	-	-	-
l. PRODSALE	-	-	.....	0.0140	0.0589	0.0272	0.00367
m. REGHOUSE	-	-	0.165	.....	.....	0.322	0.0853
n. STORE	-	-	0.237	.....	.....	.....	.....
N	74	81	224	98	303	49	337
C_{max}	0.61	0.56	0.90	0.77	0.86	0.86	0.86
C_{pro}	0.52	0.51	0.82	0.64	0.77	0.76	0.76
MC_{pro}	0.54	0.52	0.89	0.70	0.84	0.81	0.85
PCC	0.80	0.74	0.91	0.85	0.89	0.92	0.86

Figure 5-1: Estimated Regression Coefficients in the Final Logit Models, Sample Sizes and Goodness of Fit Criteria

found to be applied, thereby characterizing the decision-making pattern within the various decision categories. A more thorough discussion of the decision criteria is deferred to Section 5.3, where the criteria are related to one another, to the conditions of each, to expectations and to previous research.

The total set of findings is summarized in Figure 5-1. The two dimensions of this table represent Sections 5.2 and 5.3, respectively. Section 5.4 is, so to speak, the third dimension, as its purpose is to comprehend the findings on a higher level of understanding. Here, the findings are related to the various presuppositions of the study, both theoretical and empirical, providing the basis for some general conclusions.

The emphasis in the sections that follow is on attaining an understanding of the criteria as components of a logical and coherent pattern, whence we seek not only to identify, but also explain which criteria are used in assortment decisions. Therefore, the criteria must be coupled to various background variables which can explain and link them together - situational variables such as product group attributes and the reseller's characteristics. Hence, the contingency of the decision criteria should be clear.

To attain the fuller comprehension aimed at in the following sections, it is, furthermore, necessary that the findings of the study be related to those of the earlier study of KF's assortment building (Section 3.4) and to the general knowledge of the research field (Section 2.4). Our objective is an integral exposition.

The fact that we have the results from the previous study of KF is of great importance when interpreting the findings of the present study. The two studies deal with essentially the same object (assortment decision criteria), in the same reseller and in the same period of time. The methodologies are, however, widely divergent. (See Section 3.1.) Thus we consider the two studies as complementary, not alternatives, which means that we can gain the following advantages generally associated with this double research strategy or triangulation approach. (Jick 1979.)

- A higher degree of validity is obtained. Where the same conclusion follows from both studies, the probability that this conclusion is correct increases.
- In certain respects, the two studies produce contradictory results. This requires the researcher to make a synthesis - he has to find out whether both statements are correct under different conditions, or ascertain which of the two methodologies is the weaker in the case in question.
- With different methodologies, the two studies uncover somewhat different parts of the object under study. Hence, together they give a more complete description of the phenomenon studied.
- Through double examination, the description of the phenomenon becomes not only broader but also deeper. As the findings from the two studies are

combined, they enrich each other. New explanations and patterns emerge, which one study alone could not produce.

It should, however, also be recognized that there are certain differences between the two studies which limit the possibilities of making fruitful comparisons. The previous study did not distinguish between different decision categories, and in fact, it did not even have a clear boundary between addition and deletion decisions. Furthermore, researching decision criteria was only part of the study and, therefore, not presented in much detail.

5.2 Decision Categories

a) Acceptance/rejection of manufacturer brands
The best estimated logit model for the decision category concerning acceptance of manufacturer brand products includes three variables:

DISTRIB: If there are no distributor brands in the product group in which the new product is to be included, its chance for acceptance is greater.

PRICE: The lower the product's relative price per unit of weight or volume, the more likely it will be accepted.

CAMPAIGN: If the market introduction of the product is accompanied by a marketing campaign on the part of the supplier, the product is more likely to be accepted.

The final logit model is

logit $\hat{P}$ = 3.48 - 1.40 DISTRIB - 0.0157 PRICE + 1.41 CAMPAIGN
(1.21) (.804)   (0.00909)   (0.396)

with standard errors in parentheses. The following table shows the prob-values for one-sided testing of the regression coefficients:

H_o $\beta_{DISTRIB} = 0$ $\beta_{PRICE} = 0$ $\beta_{CAMPAIGN} = 0$
p $p \approx 0.048$ $p \approx 0.048$ $p \approx 0.000$

This indicates that the variable CAMPAIGN has a strongly positive effect on the probability of accepting the product $P(Y=1)$, while the variables DISTRIB and PRICE have a rather weak negative effect on the probability $P(Y=1)$.

The model creates the following classification table. The total number of observations in this decision category is 78, so only four observations are missing in the final model.

Number of cases	$\hat{y} = 1$	$\hat{y} = 0$	Total
$y = 1$	19	10	29
$y = 0$	5	40	45
Total	24	50	74

On the basis of this table, the goodness of fit criteria C_{max}, C_{pro}, MC_{pro} and the PCC are computed. The results are 0.61, 0.52, 0.54 and 0.80, respectively. The difference between PCC = 0.80 and MC_{pro} = 0.54 illustrates the powerful increase in the goodness of fit measure by including the predictor variables in the logit model. The model is obviously successful in describing the data. It is, however, better to correctly predict the rejection outcomes than the acceptance outcomes (40 out of 45 or 89 percent as compared to 19 out of 29 or 66 percent). All three variables are expected to be in the equation and, with only minor modifications, in accordance both with Nilsson's findings and with general knowledge about assortment decision criteria. They are logically understandable, and together, they form a coherent pattern.

The common denominator of this pattern is the profitability goal of the chain. PRICE and CAMPAIGN are expressions of the enterprise's desire to attain profits by increasing sales volume. If a product is new, there are no sales figures on which the buyers can base their decision. Instead, they have to make a sales forecast, using other variables as indicators of future sales. Price and introductory marketing campaign are very good indicators for this purpose. Most often, both of them are strongly correlated to consumer acceptance and thus to sales. They are also easy to assess, as they appear as single quantitative measures.

Also the DISTRIB criterion is strongly related to the profitability goal of the chain, though in a different way. It signifies that the reseller hesitates to accept new manufacturer brands in cases where these may lead to reduced sales of distributor brands. The latter are generally more profitable, but they have also several other positive effects - they contribute to a store image and loyalty; they make the distributor less dependent on strong suppliers, etc.

b)   Acceptance/rejection of manufacturer brands and distributor brands
Due to the internal procedures within the firm, new distributor brand products are not subject to real decision by the assortment committee. It is more a question of confirming decisions already made by a subcommittee. Consequently, as no products are rejected in that decision category, it has to be eliminated from the analysis.

Nevertheless, it is possible to add these products to those of the preceding decision category, thereby creating a new category comprising all new product decisions. In this category only two criteria are identified:

PRICE : The lower the product's relative price per unit of weight or volume, the more likely it will be accepted.

CAMPAIGN: If the market introduction of the product is accompanied by a marketing campaign on the part of the supplier, the product is more likely to be accepted.

The best logit model found is:

$$\text{logit } \hat{P} = 3.44 - 0.0214 \text{ PRICE} + 0.996 \text{ CAMPAIGN}$$
$$(1.20) \quad (0.0105) \qquad\qquad (0.316)$$

The prob-values for β_{PRICE} and $\beta_{CAMPAIGN}$ are 0.023 and 0.001, respectively.

Also in this decision category, the classification table shows a remarkable increase in the goodness of fit measures, when considering $C_{max} = 0.56$, $C_{pro} = 0.51$, $MC_{pro} = 0.52$ and PCC = 0.74. The model is again better at predicting the rejection outcomes (84 percent) than the acceptance outcomes (61 percent). The number of missing observations is six.

Number of cases	$\hat{y} = 1$	$\hat{y} = 0$	Total
$y = 1$	22	14	36
$y = 0$	7	38	45
Total	29	52	81

It is no surprise that the findings in this decision category resemble those of the preceding category, as the data sets overlap very much. Of the 87 products in this category, 78 are manufacturer brands, while nine are distributor brands.

In relation to the preceding decision category, the variable DISTRIB drops out here. This is but natural. When it comes to acceptance of distributor brand products, the reseller has no reason to be reluctant, if the product group already has one or a few distributor brands. On the contrary, it could be argued that the existence of distributor brands in the product group may support the sales of new distributor brands. This means that the distributor brands cause a counteracting tendency in relation to the manufacturer brands, explaining why the variable DISTRIB is missing here.

The rationale for applying the other two criteria in this decision category is the same as in the last one, i.e., low prices and the existence of marketing campaigns are good indicators of future sales and profits. This holds true, regardless of whether manufacturer or distributor brands are concerned.

c)   *Retention/deletion of manufacturer brands in product groups without distributor brands*

The best logit model includes the following predictor variables:

MARKLEAD: The likelihood that a manufacturer brand is retained in the assortment increases, if it is supplied by a non-market-leading company.

REGHOUSE: The greater the number of regional warehouses carrying an item, the greater the likelihood of the item remaining in the assortment.

STORE: Products recommended for large outlets only are more likely to be retained than products considered suitable for both large and small stores.

The best estimated logit model is:

$$\text{logit } \hat{P} = -1.45 \text{ MARKLEAD} + 0.165 \text{ REGHOUSE} + 0.237 \text{ STORE}$$
$$(0.520) \qquad\qquad (0.0304) \qquad\qquad (0.733)$$

Prob-values for one-sided testing of the coefficients are:

H_o	$\beta_{MARKLEAD} = 0$	$\beta_{REGHOUSE} = 0$	$\beta_{STORE} = 0$
p	$p \approx 0.004$	$p \approx 0.000$	$p \approx 0.001$

The constant term does not deviate significantly from zero.

There are 40 observations missing, and of these, 34 belong to the category $y = 1$, while 235 observations of the total (261) belong to this category. If the missing values are randomly selected, the expected number to compare with the 34 cases will be $40 \times 235/261 = 36$. The observed and expected number of cases are not very deviant.

Number of cases	$\hat{y} = 1$	$\hat{y} = 0$	Total
y = 1	201	0	201
y = 0	20	3	23
Total	221	3	224

The computed values of C_{max}, C_{pro}, MC_{pro} and PCC are 0.90, 0.82, 0.89 and 0.91, respectively. The improvement in the criteria is rather weak, but that is not unexpected, as the prior PCC measures C_{max} and MC_{pro} are as high as 0.90 and 0.89. In the classification table, it is seen that all (100%!) of the actual retention outcomes are correctly classified, while, on the other hand, the model is poor at predicting deletion outcomes - only three of the 23 decisions (13%). This finding in inversed in relation to the two preceding categories, which, however, both comprise new product decisions.

Hence, the introduction of the predictor variables in this decision category only slightly increases the proportion of correctly predicted cases. A further splitting of the data is not fruitful. Hence, this decision category is the least successful. This is probably due to a high degree of heterogeneity in the data set, which represents widely varying product groups.

The significance of the MARKLEAD variable must be understood in the light of the distributor's highly specific characteristics: a very large organization; a consumer cooperative union; a history of fierce struggles with monopolies and cartels; comprehensive production in own industries, etc. With these characteristics it is but natural that the enterprise applies a pronounced independence strategy, implying that market-leading suppliers are regarded with some caution, and their products run a greater risk of being deleted. This is further discussed in the next section.

The REGHOUSE variable is quite easy to grasp, as it is closely related to the sales figures of the product. When fewer warehouses carry a product, its sales decline, and it is dropped. On the other hand, if a product is carried by all or nearly all of the regional warehouses, the assortment committee members (most of whom are regional representatives) are not likely to argue for the deletion of the product.

To interpret the STORE variable, it is necessary, as will be shown in Section 5.3, to take the character of the products into consideration. Simply stated, products held to be suitable for both large and small stores tend to be of a standard type - large volumes, basic consumer needs, small differences between brands, etc. Such products can be and are produced by many manufacturers, as they imply high and stable sales, and they are uncomplicated to produce. This means that there is an ample supply of comparable brands, and the distributor can fairly easily shift from one supplier to another. Also, in the competition with other retail chains, it is mainly these standard products, which are of importance. This should be compared to the situation for products destined for the larger stores only. These have more often a specialty character, which means that the reseller has both more difficulty and less reason to exchange from one brand to another.

Hence, there are logical explanations for all three predictor variables.

Together, they also form a fairly coherent pattern, though perhaps not as apparent as in the other decision categories.

The core of this pattern is, again, the profitability goal of the company, but this takes different forms, depending on the time perspective. The REGHOUSE variable is, as mentioned, directly related to sales and profits. The STORE variable, interpreted as standard versus specialty products, has an intermediary link to the profitability goal, as it is economically sound to let the standard products undergo more changes than the specialty products. The MARKLEAD variable, finally, has considerable long-run implications for the market position of the distributor, and thus for economic goal attainment.

d)   Retention/deletion of manufacturer brands in product groups with distributor brands

The final logit model in this decision category includes four predictor variables:

GRPSIZE: A product's chances of remaining in the assortment increase with the number of products in the product group.

GRADSIZE: The likelihood of a product remaining in the assortment increases if the size of the product group (excluding the product in question) increases.

MARKLEAD: The likelihood of a manufacturer brand being retained in the assortment increases if it is supplied by a non-market-leading company.

PRODSALE: The more positive the sales trend of a product, the more likely the product will be retained.

The estimated logit model is given by:

$$\text{logit } \hat{P} = \underset{(0.0553)}{0.157 \text{ GRPSIZE}} + \underset{(0.152)}{0.459 \text{ GRADSIZE}}$$

$$- \underset{(0.663)}{1.26 \text{ MARKLEAD}} + \underset{(0.00612)}{0.0140 \text{ PRODSALE}}$$

Prob-values for (one-sided) testing of the coefficients are given in the following table:

H_0	$\beta_{\text{GRPSIZE}} = 0$	$\beta_{\text{GRADSIZE}} = 0$	$\beta_{\text{MARKLEAD}} = 0$	$\beta_{\text{PRODSALE}} = 0$
p	$p \simeq 0.004$	$p \simeq 0.002$	$p \simeq 0.032$	$p \simeq 0.013$

It is also seen that the constant term is excluded because of lack of significance.

The classification table of the model shows that the introduction of the four explanatory variables, as defined, increases the chance criteria from C_{max} = 0.77, C_{pro} = 0.64 and MC_{pro} = 0.70 to PCC = 0.85. Out of the 75 retention decision outcomes, no less than 73 (97%) are correctly classified, while in the deletion category only 10 of the 23 decisions (43%) are correctly predicted. Only one observation is missing.

Number of cases	$\hat{y} = 1$	$\hat{y} = 0$	Total
y = 1	73	2	75
y = 0	13	10	23
Total	86	12	98

The significance of the GRPSIZE variable can be explained as follows. All product groups contain a number of basic products (characterized by high sales figures, consumer loyalty, standard traits, a large share of the consumer's budget, many of them distributor brands, etc.) and a number of supplementary products (for special consumption occasions and for various consumer minorities, with unusual ingredients and tastes, etc.) The larger the product group, the higher the proportion of basic products. Some small product groups may even consist solely of unusual products. This distinction is relevant, because the basic products are changed less frequently than the supplementary ones. Consequently, the products of larger product groups are, on the average, deleted less often than those in smaller groups. (See Section 5.3, (b) for further elaboration.)

The reason why the GRADSIZE variable turns out to be important is that in this decision category, there is a disproportionately larger number of assortment reviews than in any other category, meaning that several products are deleted simultaneously. This category is especially relevant for assortment reviews, because in its product groups the manufacturer brands compete strongly with distributor brands, and it is rational for the committee to favor the latter. The explanation of the MARKLEAD variable is roughly the same as in the preceding decision category, i.e., the distributor has certain characteristics, such as having a comprehensive set of its own brands, which affects its relations to market-leading suppliers in a negative fashion.

Finally, the PRODSALE variable is readily understood. The product's current sales trend is the best possible indicator of its future sales and profit potential.

All in all, the predictor variables of this decision category form a pattern which has a fundamental similarity to that of the preceding category. All the criteria identified can be seen as related to the profitability goal of the enterprise, some more directly (PRODSALE), and others only indirectly (GRPSIZE, GRADSIZE and especially MARKLEAD).

There are some interesting observations to be made when comparing the last two decision categories, i.e., the deletion of manufacturer brands from product groups where, respectively, there are or are not distributor brands. In both cases, market leadership is identified as being important. So the difference between these two decision categories lies in the other criteria. In the case where the product group contains distributor brands, there are three other criteria which can be characterized as more dynamic, more product-group specific and more complex and difficult to recognize, assess and apply. In the other case, where there are no distributor brands in the product group, there are two other criteria, both static, product specific and simple.

This difference in the character of the criteria, the large difference in the retention rate (90 percent in the preceding decision category as compared to 77 per cent here) and the large number of assortment reviews in this decision category all indicate that the decision maker is more thorough in making an analysis and more critical towards manufacturer brands when distributor brands are present in the product group than when they are not. This is also completely in line with the argument, put forward in the next section, that it is logical for the distributor to support its own brands because of the substantial investments and large fixed costs involved in these products.

e)   Retention/deletion of manufacturer brands
Since this decision category is an aggregate of the two preceding ones, the findings here show certain resemblances. The predictor variables in the logit model are:

GRPSIZE: A product's chances of remaining in the assortment increase with the number of products in the product group.

GRADSIZE: The likelihood of a product remaining in the assortment increases if the size of the product group (excluding the product in question) increases.

DISTRIB: If there are no distributor brands in the product group to which the product belongs, its chances of being retained are greater.

PRODSALE: The more favorable the sales trend of a product, the more likely it will be retained.

The final logit model is as follows (no constant term):

logit $\hat{P}$ = 0.175 GRPSIZE + 0.279 GRADSIZE
(0.0327)   (0.0977)

- 0.683 DISTRIB   + 0.00589 PRODSALE
(0.345)   (0.00230)

The prob-values for the regression coefficients are (one-sided testing):

H_o $\beta_{GRPSIZE} = 0$ $\beta_{GRADSIZE} = 0$ $\beta_{DISTRIB} = 0$ $\beta_{PRODSALE} = 0$

p $p \simeq 0.000$ $p \simeq 0.003$ $p \simeq 0.025$ $p \simeq 0.006$

From the classification table we compute the chance criteria to be $C_{max} = 0.86$, $C_{pro} = 0.77$, $MC_{pro} = 0.84$ and PCC = 0.89. Again, it is seen that the model is considerably better at correctly classifying the retention outcomes (100%) than the deletion outcomes (24%).

Number of cases	$\hat{y} = 1$	$\hat{y} = 0$	Total
y = 1	261	1	262
y = 0	31	10	41
Total	292	11	303

The number of missing values is 57 (15.8%) of the total number of observations (360) in this decision category. The observed and expected number of the missing observations belonging to the category y = 1 are both 49, so no bias in the missing observations, with respect to the response variable, is found.

It is seen that three of the four criteria identified here coincide with those of the preceding category (d). The rationale is largely the same. Likewise, the entire pattern of criteria in this decision category is basically the same as in the preceding one.

The fact that the variable DISTRIB turned out to be important is a consequence of the general differences between the two constituent categories (c) and (d), where this variable is rendered irrelevant by the category definitions. The explanation of its significance parallels the one given in decision category (a), acceptance of new manufacturer brands. For the distributor, it is rational to favor its own brands, whence it is more prone to delete manufacturer brands that are competing with distributor brands than those that are not.

One might find it surprising that the findings of this decision category deviate considerably from the one without distributor brands (c), which comprises 231 products as opposed to only 98 in the category with distributor brands (d). The most likely reason for this skewness is that the findings of the latter (d) are more clear-cut, while the former (c) gives fairly inconclusive results - its proportion of correctly predicted decisions is, in fact, increased very little by the inclusion of predictor variables.

f)   Retention/deletion of distributor brands

The best estimated logit model for this decision category includes two predictor variables:

PRODSALE: The more favorable the sales trend of a product, the more likely it will be retained.

REGHOUSE: The greater the number of regional warehouses carrying an item, the more likely it will remain in the assortment.

The final logit model is given by:

$$\text{logit } \hat{P} = -4.96 \quad + 0.0272 \text{ PRODSALE} \quad + 0.322 \text{ REGHOUSE,}$$
$$\qquad\qquad (2.49) \quad (0.0191) \qquad\qquad (0.141)$$

Prob-values for one-sided testing of the hypothesis, $\beta_{\text{PRODSALE}} = 0$ and $\beta_{\text{REGHOUSE}} = 0$ are 0.084 and 0.014, respectively. The coefficient of the variable PRODSALE is found to be only weakly significant, but as the variable is given high priority, it is included in the final logit model.

The different chance criteria to be compared with the PCC = 0.92 for this model, including the predictor variables PRODSALE and REGHOUSE, are $C_{\text{max}} = 0.86$, $C_{\text{pro}} = 0.76$ and $MC_{\text{pro}} = 0.81$. From the classification table, it also follows that the classification of the actual retention outcomes is perfect (100%), while only three of the seven deletions are correctly predicted (43%).

Number of cases	$\hat{y} = 1$	$\hat{y} = 0$	Total
y = 1	42	0	42
y = 0	4	3	7
Total	46	3	49

There are ten missing values, all belonging to the class y = 1. The expected number in this class, if the missing cases were randomly distributed, is found to be 10 x 52/59 = 9. The observed and expected numbers are quite similar.

The two criteria are clearly related to the sales goal of the distributor, thus also to its profitability goal. Old distributor brands are deleted when their market positions have been irrevocably weakened. Of all the potential explanatory variables included in this study, these two are the most evident expressions of a product's market position, thus also indicators of future sales and profit potential.

The conclusion is that the enterprise eliminates its own brands, when the demand for them becomes so weak that their profit potential is lost. Other factors, like the price of the product, the sales trend or the composition of the product group, cannot to any significant degree save a distributor brand in the face of shrinking demand. Manufacturer brands may be deleted for a variety of reasons, while distributor brands remain in the assortment until their prospects for the future are definitively exhausted. The logic of this decision rule is all the clearer, if we recognize that lower sales not only mean less revenue; they also mean that various overhead costs have to be covered by fewer units, which causes the per unit profit to decline more sharply.

The two significant criteria have characteristics that make them quite easy to identify, interpret and evaluate. They are both expressed in simple, ready-at-hand figures. Furthermore, they are product specific variables, as opposed to product group specific or product group related. This, too, makes them easy to apply. Product group specific variables, such as the sales trend of the product group, and product related variables, such as the product's share of the total sales of the product group, require more probing deliberations and/or additional calculations, hence, they imply more complicated decision making. All this indicates that decisions concerning deletion of distributor brands, are comparatively easy to make.

g) *Retention/deletion of manufacturer and distributor brands*

In this decision category there are five predictor variables in the best logit model:

GRPSIZE: A product's likelihood of remaining in the assortment increases with the number of products in the product group.

GRADSIZE: The likelihood of a product remaining in the assortment increases if the size of the product group (excluding the product in question) increases.

DISTRIB: The likelihood of a product remaining in the assortment is greater, if the relevant product group does not contain any distributor brands.

PRODSALE: The more favorable the sales trend of a product, the more likely it will be retained.

REGHOUSE: The greater the number of regional warehouses carrying an item, the more likely it will remain in the assortment.

The final logit model is defined by:

$$\text{logit } \hat{P} = \underset{(0.0300)}{0.105 \text{ GRPSIZE}} + \underset{(0.0896)}{0.189 \text{ GRADSIZE}}$$

$$- \underset{(0.346)}{0.691 \text{ DISTRIB}} + \underset{(0.00227)}{0.00367 \text{ PRODSALE}} + \underset{(0.0253)}{0.0853 \text{ REGHOUSE}}$$

The prob-values are given by:

H_o $\text{ß}_{GRPSIZE}=0$ $\text{ß}_{GRADSIZE}=0$ $\text{ß}_{DISTRIB}=0$ $\text{ß}_{PRODSALE}=0$ $\text{ß}_{REGHOUSE}=0$

p $p \simeq 0.000$ $p \simeq 0.019$ $p \simeq 0.021$ $p \simeq 0.054$ $p \simeq 0.000$

The chance criteria C_{max}, C_{pro} and MC_{pro} and PCC for including the five predictor variables in the model are 0.86, 0.76, 0.85 and 0.86, respectively. In this decision category, we find an extremely skew ability of the model to correctly predict the two types of decision outcome - 99 percent of the retentions and six percent of the deletions are correctly classified.

Number of cases	$\hat{y} = 1$	$\hat{y} = 0$	Total
y = 1	287	3	290
y = 0	44	3	47
Total	331	6	337

The total number of observations is 419, so the number of missing values here is 82 or 19.6 percent. This high value is a consequence of the rather large number (five) of predictor variables in this model. The observed and expected number of missing values in the y = 1 category is found to be 73 and 71, respectively.

This decision category is an aggregation of the two preceding ones, so it is natural that the identified criteria are a mixture of those presented above. As all these variables have already been discussed, there is no reason to elaborate further upon them here.

The pattern of criteria applied in deletion decisions deviates from that of the addition decisions, i.e., category b. (See Figure 5-1.) To explain the deletion decisions, it takes three product group variables and two product specific variables, while one product related and one product specific variable are enough for the addition decision. In the case of deletions, the products in a given product group are, in a way, intertwined, so the committee has to make a deeper analysis. In addition cases, the product has no relations to current products, and it is difficult to foretell what effect an addition will have on the rest of the assortment. Thus, the sales prospects of the product, induced by a favorable price and marketing campaign, become the sole decisive factor. These differences indicate that it is a more complicated task making decisions about old products than about new ones.

5.3 Decision Criteria

a) GRPSALE

It was expected that the variable GRPSALE would be rather important in connection with both acceptance and deletion decisions. The sales trend of the total product group would seem to be an indicator for the future sales volume of products belonging to this group. If sales are increasing, the decision makers would be more prone to accept new products. They would try to exploit current market trends, among other things, by introducing new varieties of taste and package size. Likewise, they would reduce the assortment in product groups with declining sales volumes. As the average sales per product decline, costs increase sharply, but can be kept down by product deletions.

These expectations are based mainly on the previous study of KF's assortment decisions, and they are also supported by other reports. In the present study, however, the sales trend of the product group proves to be of no significance, either for acceptance or for deletion decisions.

We can find two alternative explanations for why this expected correlation fails to appear. Firstly, there may simply be no link between the sales increase of a product group and a propensity to enlarge it. On the contrary, the distributor might use a tactic of "never change a winning team." Making changes might be risky, and perhaps unnecessary. Moreover, wider assortments are always costly.

An alternative explanation is that, contrary to expectation, there is no correlation between a product group's declining sales and a reduction in size. Buyers do not passively look on, as sales begin to drop. They may well try to break the trend by making some switches in the product mix, i.e., by making addition decisions as well as deletion decisions. If this occurs regularly, any positive correlations between the product group's sales trend and the likely occurrence of acceptance and deletion decisions is blurred.

It is impossible to say anything about the validity of these two hypothetical explanations, but they both seem reasonable. This uncertainty might have been overcome, if we had split the GRPSALE variable in two, i.e., one for a rising product group sales trend, and another for a declining trend. This problem was, however, unforeseen when the study was planned.

b) GRPSIZE

It was thought that the variable GRPSIZE might have some importance, as the distributor could be expected to take a more reluctant attitude toward expanding already large product groups or reducing already small ones. Likewise, large product groups are usually more unstable than smaller ones. On the other hand, it should be recognized that the concept of size is very much dependent on the product group in question. For example, seven varieties of frozen spinach would be considered as a large product group, while seven varieties of cans of pickled herring would be a very small product group.

Against this background, the size of the product group was not expected to be of any significance. Neither the previous study of KF nor general knowledge of assortment decision criteria indicated otherwise.

This expectation proved to be correct for the acceptance decisions and for several decision categories with regard to deletions. The main exception is category (d), deletions of manufacturer brands when there are distributor brands in the product group. In this category, the correlation is even so strong that it also shows up in the totals, both for all manufacturer brand deletions and for the grand total of deletions.

The direction of the correlation is also somewhat remarkable. It denotes that the larger the product group, the more likely will the products remain in the assortment, which is contrary to what would be most probable.

On closer examination, however, a plausible explanation emerges. The product groups in this decision category consist of a small number of distributor brands plus a varying number of manufacturer brands. Most often, the distributor brands constitute the "core" of the product group, i.e., they are the products with the largest and most stable sales. It is KF's policy to produce mainly such high-volume, standard products. The manufacturer brands serve as supplements, adding variants of tastes, sizes, packages, price alternatives, etc. to the product group.

Product groups with few items generally also have low sales volumes. In order to maintain reasonably large sales for each separate product, the number of products must be kept down. This is valid especially for the distributor brands. As these are sold only through KF's own outlets, they must have fairly large sales volumes. As a consequence, it becomes very important to reduce the number of manufacturer brands, if the product group is small. The smaller the product group, the more the relative importance of the distributor brands, and the more inclined is the committee to keep the number of manufacturer brands down.

A supplementary explanation might be based on the character of the product groups, large and small. Larger product groups often correspond to consumer demand that is substantial and varied. This means that the products are important to the consumers, thus also to the distributor. There are many closely related variants of taste, size and packages. This means that the product mix is carefully composed and that it is difficult to make any changes, for example, deletions, without serious consequences for the appeal of the entire product group. The opposite is often true of smaller product groups. Here there are few interrelations between the products. The product group is of less importance for consumers and for the distributor. Deleting products from such product groups does not have very far-reaching effects.

To this line of reasoning may be added that KF's own products do not play an identical role in the more important (larger) and the less important (smaller) product groups. In the former, the distributor brands generally already have a strong position, while in the latter they are weaker. So in order to protect the distributor brands, the committee is more apt to delete manufacturer brands from the small product groups than from the large ones.

There is still one more explanation which is possible, though quite speculative. It relates to the fact that there is a large number of assortment reviews in this decision category. It can be argued that an assortment review in a large product group leads to the elimination of relatively few items, because the committee, during the preceding regular assortment decisions, has been more careful not to let the already large product group expand any further. If the product group is smaller, the committee has not had the same prior opportunity to become so restrictive towards additions of new products, so there is more accumulated "fat" to trim.

No matter which of these explanations is true, it can be concluded that the association between the decision and the product group size is spurious. It is not the product group size in itself, which is important, but some structural characteristics of the product group, related to its size.

c) GRADSIZE

For several of the explanatory variables, we can identify counteractive tendencies which make it difficult to foretell their probable effects. This is true for the variable GRADSIZE.

On the one hand, distributors generally tend to apply an "one in, one out" principle in their assortment building, in order to prevent their assortment from increasing too much in size. According to the previous study of KF, this rule-of-thumb is very strongly internalized in KF's decision makers. This means that there should be negative correlations between decision outcomes and the GRADSIZE variable. The likelihood of a new product being accepted should be greater, if a current product is simultaneously deleted, and vice versa.

On the other hand, there are also situations where several products are accepted simultaneously or deleted simultaneously, so the association between the decision outcome and the GRADSIZE variable is positive. The first such situation occurs when a supplier presents a whole range of new products; and as there are interrelations between the products with regard to demand and handling, the distributor accepts many, or even all, of them.

The second situation is connected with the so-called assortment reviews, which are conducted once or twice a year. In these, the decision makers scrutinize specific product groups, in order to streamline the assortment and reduce the number of items. The aim of the assortment reviews is to counteract the tendency toward creeping product group growth, which is inherent in regular assortment building. Hence, in an assortment review it is normal that several products are deleted without any being accepted. This means that there is a positive correlation between one product's likelihood of being deleted and that of other products.

In the literature on assortment decision making, assortment reviews are mentioned only by a few authors. In KF, they are, however, conducted quite regularly, and according to the previous study of KF, they play an important role in its assortment building.

Against this background, it is quite understandable that the change in product group size proves to be of importance in only one of the basic decision categories. There is a positive association in the category where manufacturer brand products are deleted from product groups which include distributor brands (d). This correlation is also seen in the two totals for deletion decisions, (e) and (g). It shows that two or more products are deleted simultaneously, which indicates the occurrence of assortment reviews.

In our data set, assortment reviews occur most frequently in this decision category. No less than 23 percent of all current products are deleted. By way of comparison, 12 percent are deleted in the distributor brand category (f) and 10 percent in the category comprising manufacturer brands in product groups without distributor brands (c).

The reason for this difference can be understood from the discussion of the preceding variable, GRPSIZE. There are manufacturer brands competing with some distributor brands, and the latter are quite sensitive to sales reductions because of the organization's heavy investments in production facilities, which entail large fixed costs. Therefore, it is especially important in this decision category to make sure that the assortments in the product groups are not expanded with too many slow-selling manufacturer brands. Assortment reviews often have the effect of leaving distributor brands in a stronger position, as it is mainly manufacturer brands competing with KF's own brands, which are eliminated.

In the decision categories (c) and (f), we believe that the variable GRADSIZE does not prove important, because the two aforementioned counteractive tendencies neutralize each other. The effect of the assortment reviews and the effect of the "one in, one out" principle are of approximately equal strength. Consequently, we consider the GRADSIZE variable to be more important than our findings show, and we still assert that the "one in, one out" principle is applied in routine decision making.

In a retrospect, it would have been wise to treat the assortment reviews as a separate decision category, since the committee seems to apply at least partially different norms in these cases.

d) DISTRIB

If a new manufacturer brand is being considered for inclusion in a product group, its chances of being accepted are smaller, when the group contains distributor brands. Likewise, as has been shown in the preceding discussions, manufacturer brands run a greater risk of being deleted, if there are distributor brands in the product group. This is an observation often made in research reports on assortment building, and the previous study of KF found the relationship to be quite distinct.

From a distributor perspective, it is entirely logical to support one's own products in this way. The manufacturer brands are the suppliers' concern. Similarly, someone has to promote the sales of the distributor brands, and there is no one else but the distributor to do so.

If manufacturer brands are added to the assortment, the sales of competing distributor brands are bound to suffer. This may often have detrimental effects on the distributor's net profits because of greatly different cost structures for manufacturer and distributor brands. The fixed costs of distributing manufacturer brands are minimal, and the variable costs are high, while distributor brands entail very large fixed costs and quite small variable costs.

Therefore, even a moderate decline in the sales of its own brands, due to competing manufacturer brands, may be detrimental to the distributor. Large per unit profits fall off, while the fixed costs incurred by heavy investments in factories, machines, personnel, etc. remain unchanged. Hence, a quite small decline in sales could result in a sizable profit reduction. This cannot be offset by the profits attained from the sales of the competing manufacturer brand, since the per unit profit is too low.

Consequently, distributors are generally very sensitive to changes in the volume of their own brands, but not of manufacturer brands. It is of great importance that the production capacity of the distributor's own factories is kept at a high level, so that the large fixed costs can be spread over a great number of units, thus ensuring high net profit per unit.

In addition, distributor brands are often of great strategic value to the distributor. They are effective instruments for market positioning in relation to competitors. They are a means of maintaining independence in relation to large suppliers. They are the basis for offering products with very specific characteristics to the consumers. All these advantages are of importance to KF, especially as a consumer cooperative.

The relevance of this criterion, the presence of distributor brands in the group, is, however, strongly dependent on how closely the manufacturer brands compete with the distributor brands. In many cases, the two may be direct substitutes, so the presence of distributor brands will completely exclude manufacturer brands. In other cases, the degree of competition may be smaller. One could even imagine that in some situations a manufacturer brand supports the sales of distributor brands in the same product group. For example, the manufacturer brand might serve as a supplement, making the entire product group more attractive to the consumers. This tendency might help to explain why this criterion turns out to be relatively weakly supported by the data.

The same counteractive tendency also explains why the presence of distributor brands in a product group has a greater impact on acceptance decisions than on deletion decisions. The manufacturer brands which are already in the assortment are there because they are well adapted to the product mix, including the distributor brands, so there is less reason to delete them. New manufacturer brands are, on the contrary, seldom well adapted to the current assortment; consequently, they run a greater risk of being rejected.

e)   PRICE

The price of the product turns out to be important in acceptance decisions, but insignificant in deletion decisions. This accords very well with both the previous study of KF and the general state of knowledge of assortment building.

This difference between acceptance and deletion decisions is readily understood, when related to the profitability of the enterprise. If an old product is selling well, it may remain in the assortment, no matter whether its price is high or low. It can even be advantageous to the distributor that there is a strong demand for an expensive product, if the net profit per unit is higher. Thus, if there is a profit to be made, price need not be decisive.

When it comes to acceptance decisions, the conditions are quite different. There are no sales figures and no established consumer loyalty to a new product. So the buyers have to make some kind of forecast. One indicator of future sales and profit potential is the price of the product compared to similar products in the product group. This is also a very important indicator, as there is a strong relationship between price and sales, and as the price variable is one of the very few which are expressed in easily understood, quantitative measures.

Another plausible reason why the price criterion is more important in decisions on new products than on old ones, is that there might, in fact, be a difference between the price levels for new and old products. If the suppliers tend to price their new products higher than the old ones, it is quite understandable that the reseller pays more attention to the new product prices. The suppliers may have several motives for such a pricing policy: a desire to raise the overall profit level; an expectation of lower consumer price sensitivity for new products; a conception of less competition for new products; a wish to cover product development costs quickly.

f) SIZE

In none of the decision categories does the package size of the product prove to be of any importance. This is in perfect accordance with expectations; neither general knowledge of assortment building nor the previous study of KF attribute much significance to this variable. According to Nilsson's study of KF, it could be effective only in rare instances. For example, a new product may be rejected, if its package is too large for the store shelves. Furthermore, there are no known trends towards larger or smaller packages.

Nevertheless, one cannot exclude the possibility that this variable could have displayed a certain influence, if it had been operationalized in a different way. The distributor presumably desires a certain balance between different package sizes in each product group. Hence, the package size could have been expressed by a code indicating whether the product represents a unique size class, a size class shared with a few other products or a size class common to many other products. One could also relate these size classes to their respective sales figures. Defining the variable in this way would probably be more relevant than the one presently used, but it would, on the other hand, be both more uncertain and more costly.

g) NEWNESS

According to previous research, a new product's degree of uniqueness is considered to be a very important criterion. The earlier study of KF reaches a similar conclusion. If a new product is very different from current products, and favorably so, it most probably will be accepted. Slight innovations, however, have no significant effect.

In this study, the NEWNESS variable fails to prove of any significance for acceptance decisions. One plausible explanation of this is that there might be few products with really unique characteristics in our data set. If this is true, the conclusions reached in the previous study are, at least, not contradicted.

An alternative, but equally possible, explanation is that unique characteristics can be evaluated differently, and this leads to inconclusive results. A unique product never leaves the decision makers indifferent. On the contrary, new features are always important in the evaluation of the product. But the outcome of this evaluation may be negative as well as positive. Either the product is rejected because of some undesirable unique characteristics, or, if these characteristics are deemed attractive, they contribute strongly to an acceptance decision.

When operationalizing the NEWNESS variable, it was not possible to take these two contradictory tendencies into consideration. That would require splitting the NEWNESS variable into two on the basis of desirable and undesirable features; and above all, it would imply much more uncertainty in the coding and require additional resources to carry out the study.

h) SHARE

The findings show that when an old product is deleted, it does not matter whether this product accounts for a small or a large share of the total sales of the product group. This holds true for all the relevant decision categories.

This seems, at first glance, quite surprising, as it is not immediately consistent with the sales and profitability goal of the distributor. According to previous research, sales are the prime concern in the distributors' assortment decisions. Here, however, the results show that products which dominate their product groups may be deleted, and marginal products may be retained.

A closer look, however, reveals an underlying logic, provided that the character of the product is taken into account. In the evaluation of a product's sales figures, the decision makers must compare them to a reasonable sales volume for this specific product. Normally, a product group is comprised of widely varied products, some of which are standard products representing a large share of the sales, while others are more distinctive. Even though the latter have a smaller share of the product group's total sales, they are necessary to give variety to the assortment, and they cannot be eliminated.

In a given product group, for example, there might be a product which should have about half of the total sales volume because of its standard character. If its sales shrink to one third, it should be replaced. Likewise, in the same product group there might be an item which is so special that only a five percent share of the product group's total sales figures is considered reasonable.

In principle, it would have been possible to take this problem into account when operationalizing the variable SHARE, for example, by splitting the product groups into new, more homogeneous subgroups on the basis of the character of the products. In practice, however, this would have been impossible, as it would have required an immense knowledge of the trade, and still, the codings would have been very uncertain.

i) MARKLEAD

The supplier's identity is generally considered to be a very important criterion, and one would expect to find this confirmed in the case of KF. Distributors tend to prefer products from large suppliers with a good reputation, broad assortments, good marketing and product development skills, high consumer loyalty, strong brand images, etc. Distributing products from these suppliers is often good business, because the suppliers are able to attain high sales volumes and high consumer traffic.

In the present study, attention is focused on the central element in the concept of supplier identity, viz., whether the supplier is a market leader or not. Previous research indicates that the market leader is more likely to have its new products accepted, and is likewise less likely to have its old products deleted. This is generally true also in the case of KF, but as will be shown below, there are some countervailing factors, which can lead to the opposite net outcome.

The findings show that supplier identity is not a significant criterion in addition decisions (a and b), nor in the aggregates of deletion decisions (e and g). When it comes to deletions of manufacturer brands (c and d), it proves important, but the relationship is negative, i.e., market leaders tend to get their old products deleted more often than non-market-leading suppliers.

The explanation of these findings is that the generally recognized orientation of distributors toward market-leading suppliers can be counteracted by a number of minor factors, which, taken together, can have quite a strong impact, especially in KF's circumstances. Each of these factors requires some discussion:

(1) Because of the small size of the Swedish market, most industries are dominated by only a few large manufacturers. KF has, on many occasions throughout its history, learned that it must be careful to safeguard its independence. Hence, the frequently observed policy of avoiding dependence on large suppliers is very manifest in KF. KF has learned this the hard way, through numerous conflicts with cartels and monopolies, especially in its earlier history. Therefore, KF tends to take a cautious attitude toward the most powerful suppliers, i.e., the market leaders.

(2) Moreover, market leaders often have other drawbacks as suppliers. It is difficult to reach advantageous agreements because of their strong negotiation position. It is also difficult for the distributor to retain control of the product mix and flow, once the leading suppliers establish a strong foothold.

(3) KF has many production units of its own, which manufacture numerous distributor brands, many of which compete with the products of the market leaders. Hence, the market leaders are not only suppliers to KF (in its wholesale function) but also competitors (in its manufacturing function), and quite often they are the strongest competitors. As KF must look after its own brands, it is natural that several market leaders' products are eliminated more often than others (in decision category d).

(4) The market leader usually has several products in the product group in question. Consequently, if a product is to be deleted, there is a greater probability that it will be one of the market leader's products.

(5) As mentioned above, the market leader is generally a large and dynamic producer. It is active and very skilled in product development and marketing,

tending by itself to eliminate its old products when they no longer satisfy its often high standards of profitability. In this way, it eases the acceptance of its new, better and more profitable products. Furthermore, the market leader is in the vanguard of technological and marketing-science development, which means that its products tend to have a relatively short life span. It is continually making product improvements and frequently introduces new products.

All of these factors are no doubt operative. Against this background, it is not surprising that market-leading suppliers tend to have their products deleted more often than others. It is also understandable that this criterion has a greater impact in product groups with distributor brands. This is an effect of factors (1) - (3).

j)   OWNPROD

The decision criterion OWNPROD is relevant only in the two main decision categories, i.e., all acceptance decisions and all rejection decisions. The reason for this is that this variable is used to define the other decision categories, figuring in these as a constant.

The findings show that OWNPROD has little significance in either of the categories. Whether the product is a distributor brand or a manufacturer brand does not affect its chances of being accepted or retained.

With regard to decisions on old products (category g), this finding is but natural. In the two constituent decision categories, retention of manufacturer brands (e) and of distributor brands (f), the proportion of products retained is about the same, viz. 86 percent and 88 percent, respectively. (See Figure 3-4.) As for the decision category involving new products (b), there is a considerable difference between acceptance rates for manufacturer and for distributor brands, viz., 38 percent and 100 percent. The number of distributor brands (9) is, however, so small in comparison to the number of manufacturer brands (78), that this difference is blurred when the two categories are merged.

k)   CAMPAIGN

In previous research, the supplier's introductory marketing campaign is considered the crucial criterion in new product decisions. In the previous study of KF's assortment building, it is, however, claimed that this variable is important only under certain conditions: if it is expected to be followed up by effective, continual marketing efforts; if it can be interpreted as a sign of the supplier's faith in its new product; and if the price and the other characteristics of the product are satisfactory.

The findings of the present study lend heavy support to the general pattern. The assurance of introductory campaigns is a most decisive criterion. To what extent it accords with the previous study of KF is difficult to say, as our methodology does not allow for any test of the provisos mentioned there. One tentative conclusion is that the CAMPAIGN variable proves important, because the three conditions are very often satisfied in our data set. Alternatively, the conclusions of the previous study might be too restrictive, possibly because the subject matter is a sensitive area for qualitative research.

l) PRODSALE

Logically, the sales trend of a current product should be expected to be the principal criterion for deletion decisions. The sales trend is equivalent to the product's market position, and it is the decision makers' best indicator of the item's future sales and profit potential. Furthermore, this should hold true for both distributor and manufacturer brands. If a product shows a declining sales curve, it is bound to be deleted, while stable, and especially increasing sales mean that the product is likely to remain in the assortment. Results from previous research are also entirely consonant with this view, as are the conclusions from the earlier study of KF.

The findings of the present study largely confirm this eminently logical variable. The product's sales trend proves to be an essential criterion in all categories of deletion decisions, except for one, viz., deletions of manufacturer brands when there are no distributor brands in the product group. Evidently, the committee treats the sales figures of a manufacturer brand in different ways according to whether there are distributor brands in the product group or not. If there are no distributor brands, the manufacturer brand's sales trend becomes unimportant as a criterion.

A bit of speculative imagination may be required to explain this. Assuming that product groups which include distributor brands are watched more closely, a decline in the sales trend of a manufacturer brand in the same group will be quickly discovered, while the possibility of an adverse effect on the group's distributor brands will lend urgency to a decision. In this context the manufacturer brand is highly vulnerable to a deletion decision, given the distributor's primary concern for its own brands. If, on the other hand, there are no distributor brands in the product group, a "wait-and-see" tactic is a more sensible reaction to a sales drop of a manufacturer brand. The need for immediate action is smaller. A hasty decision might turn out to be unnecessary, as sales often increase again. It would also lead to extra costs and trouble without any benefits to distributor brands.

m) REGHOUSE

This variable has not been directly defined as a decision variable in any of the previous studies, not even in the earlier study of KF. As it is very closely related to the sales volumes of the products, it could, however, be of considerable significance for the decision outcomes. To be more precise, this variable expresses the general importance that a product is considered to have within its product group. Products which are important because of, e.g., high sales, high complementarity to other products or distinctive image, are most often distributed through all or nearly all of the regional warehouses, and for them, the risk of being deleted is small. Furthermore, the reseller must face reduced economies of scale in the handling of the product, if warehouse coverage declines. Consequently, there should be a high positive correlation between a product's remaining in the assortment and the number of warehouses carrying it.

This expectation is strongly supported by the data. Both in the aggregate of all deletion decisions (g) and the two decision categories regarding distributor brands (f) and manufacturer brands in product groups with no distributor brands (c), this variable turns out to be very decisive.

On the other hand, the number of warehouses carrying an item does not prove significant for deletions of manufacturer brands when there are distributor brands in the product group (d), nor for the sum of manufacturer brand deletions (e). At first glance, this might seem surprising, but a closer examination shows that there is a fully logical explanation.

KF's own products are generally carried by all the 17 regional warehouses. If the number of warehouses distributing an item falls only moderately, say to 13, this is a strong indicator that the product is problematical. The production volume is sharply reduced, with a resultant sharp rise in average costs.

When, on the other hand, it is a question of a manufacturer brand competing with KF's own brands, the situation is, in a way, reversed. Such an item is vulnerable, despite high warehouse coverage. Actually, the very fact that the manufacturer brand is successful could induce KF to develop a similar brand of its own, and then the pioneer manufacturer brand is dropped. There are several examples of this in our data set. Likewise, many product groups consist of a core of a few distributor brands supplemented by a number of manufacturer brands. Among the latter are some which have low warehouse coverage, but, nevertheless, they may remain in the assortment, because their supplementary role is considered valuable.

Finally, there is the decision category with manufacturer brands in product groups where there are no distributor brands, and here the situation is again reversed. As KF has none of its own brands to safeguard, it fully appreciates manufacturer brands with high warehouse coverage, as this ensures a certain economy of scale. Consequently, the number of regional warehouses carrying an item is positively correlated with the item's remaining in the assortment.

n) STORE
There is no inherent reason to expect this variable to be of any significance as a decision criterion. The previous study of KF did not find it so, and in other studies there is nothing that corresponds to this variable. Likewise, it does not seem sensible that the distributor should favor a particular store size.

Nevertheless, the variable STORE proves significant in one decision category, viz., deletion of manufacturer brands when there are no distributor brands in the product group. If the item is sold only in the largest stores, the risk of being deleted is minor, while the opposite holds true for products recommended for both large and small stores.

This finding cannot be understood on the basis of store sizes only. It is rather an effect of some links between the products' suitability for certain store sizes and some other characteristics of the products, such as their competitive positions and whether they are standard items or specialties. Products which are distinctive and specialized are often recommended only for the larger stores, and there they do not face very stiff competition. This is the case, for example, with items in extremely large packages, and items for special occasions or for certain minority groups. Standard products with large sales volumes, on the other hand, are found in stores of all sizes. Because of their large sales volumes and their standard character, there are many manufacturers who are willing and able to produce them. Hence, there is an ample supply of standard products which are close substitutes.

Consequently, the standard products face considerably harder competition than the specialty products. This is true of the relation between various standard products within a specific product group of a single distributor, as well as between different distributors. It could be added that in competition between distributors, it is mainly the standard products which count, because of their large volumes and their great importance both for household budgets and distributor profits. It is of utmost importance for the distributor that he has the "right" standard products in his assortment. As for specialty items, there are no "right" products because of substantial heterogeneity in both supply and demand; they also have less profit potential for the distributor.

In this light, it seems quite logical that manufacturer brands suitable for both large and small stores, i.e., standard products, run a greater risk of being deleted from product groups where there are no distributor brands. In the adjacent decision category, viz., deletion of manufacturer brands from product groups with distributor brands, the conditions are different. The distributor brands are usually sold in both large and small stores, while the manufacturer brands tend to be sold only in larger stores. With the distributor brands' generally lower risk of deletion, this gives rise to a counteractive tendency, which explains why there, in this decision category, is no correlation between the store size variable and the decision outcomes.

In retrospect, this variable should have been operationalized differently. It is reasonable to assume that the decision makers try to attain a balance between products suitable for small stores, average-size stores and large stores. Consequently, the variable could also have been defined by whether the store class has only one item, several items or many items in a given product group. It could then be hypothesized that the product would have a good chance of being retained, if it falls in the first category, and a poorer chance, if in the third category.

5.4 Conclusions

Criteria which are significant for decision outcomes have been identified in each of the decision categories presented in the preceding sections. Proportionately more correct predictions were made with the use of these criteria than would have been possible without them.

For some of the decision categories, notably the largest and most heterogeneous ones (categories c, e and g), the improvement of predictive ability is admittedly not very great. Nevertheless, we consider the findings satisfactory, considering the various input limitations of the study, even if it is impossible to determine the extent to which the limitations of the data set and the variables affect the results.

- The study is based exclusively on the product fact sheets. These constitute only one of six information sources available to the decision makers, though certainly the most important one. (See Section 3.5.) This means that certain types of information are necessarily excluded, such as the decision makers' personal experience and evaluation of the product, the buyers' oral presentation of the products to the committee, the products' sales results or sales prospects in different regions, and the decision makers' specific appraisal of the various suppliers.
- It was not possible to utilize all of the information supplied by the product fact sheets. (See Section 3.7.) We especially regret that the test panel results had to be omitted, due to incomplete registration on the part of the buyers. The previous study of KF shows that this variable is an important criterion when a new product is considered for acceptance and an old product is to be replaced by a new one.
- Operationalizing the variables unavoidably entails some uncertainties. In the preceding section (5.3), we mention alternative operationalizations of the variables GRPSALE, GRADSIZE, SIZE, NEWNESS and SHARE. Likewise, as can be seen in Section 3.7, there are other ways of defining the variable PRICE, i.e., it could have been expressed as price per package rather than price per unit of volume or weight. Finally, there is inevitably a significant subjective element in the codings of the variables NEWNESS, MARKLEAD and PRICE.

There are strikingly great differences in the logit models' predictive ability, depending on the type of outcome. In new product decisions, the logit models succeed in predicting rejection outcomes better (89% and 84%) than acceptance outcomes (66% and 61%). In the decision categories involving old products, the logit models predict retentions far better (97% - 100%) than deletions (6% - 43%).

To explain these differences, we refer to what is said in Section 1.3 about the resellers' inherently conservative attitude towards assortment changes. Rejecting new products and retaining old ones are, so to speak, the normal decisions, and for these there are relatively stable and few criteria. The researcher thus finds it easy to accurately identify these criteria. New product acceptance and old product deletion, on the other hand, can have such profound consequences for the reseller that the decision makers apply many and varied criteria. This heterogeneity means that it becomes more difficult to uncover the criteria when the decisions result in acceptance or deletion.

In the preceding sections, we have presented explanations of all the criteria identified in all the decision categories. It must be acknowledged, however, that these explanations contain some speculative elements. This is especially true for the decision criteria pertaining to retention/deletion of manufacturer brands. But given the incomplete knowledge of intermediate variables, some elements of imaginative reasoning are necessary, if there is to be any explanation. The explanation must, however, be plausible.

The explanations delineate logical and coherent patterns for each decision category as well as for all the categories as a whole. Furthermore, we have throughout the presentations in the preceding section related our findings to those of the previous study of KF and the general state of knowledge of reseller assortment decision criteria. We have found them congruent on most of the points where comparisons are feasible. The main deviation pertains to the significance of supplier marketing campaigns. In the present study, this variable is found to be the crucial criterion for acceptance decisions, and this accords with most previous research. The earlier study of KF, however, concluded that the introductory marketing campaign is of only moderate importance. As was explained in Section 5.3, we consider this difference to be due to some weaknesses in the qualitative methodology used in that study.

The common denominator of all the decision category patterns is profitability. The whole process of assortment building can be regarded as a continual striving for profitability. As the conditions, however, vary from one decision category to the other, the profitability goal is manifested in different ways. For example, one set of criteria is applied to attain profitability in assortment decisions involving distributor brands, and another set is used when manufacturer brands are involved.

As explained in Section 1.4, an ultimate goal, located at the top of a goal hierarchy, cannot directly determine specific decisions. These must be guided by decision criteria which are found at the bottom of the goal hierarchy. Hence, the ultimate goal must be operationalized, generally through a series of intermediate steps. In this trickle-down process of operationalization, the ultimate goal can take many concrete forms. The criteria used for one type of decision might deviate considerably from those used for another decision type.

These variations are not arbitrary; on the contrary, they are quite systematic. They depend on the conditions characterizing the type of decision.

If two decisions are made under the same or very similar conditions, the decision maker operationalizes his ultimate goal through identical criteria patterns.

This situational or contingency approach can explain several traits:

- The identification of different sets of criteria in different decision categories depends on the fact that these decision categories have different characteristics. This has been explained in the preceding sections.
- In certain decision categories, especially those regarding manufacturer brands, we did not succeed in significantly raising the proportion of correct predictions by including the identified criteria. The reason for this might be that these decision categories are too heterogeneous, i.e., the differences between the conditions of different product decisions are too great. Furthermore, there are very high prior PCC's for these decision categories.
- As was shown in the literature survey in Chapter 2, the findings of previous research constitute a very heterogeneous body of knowledge, from which it is difficult to extract any generally valid conclusions. The reason for this is that the various studies deal with assortment decisions made under greatly varying conditions.

In the present study, some of these conditions are explicitly tested. Hence, we find that different sets of criteria are applied, depending on whether the decision affects new or old products, manufacturer brands or distributor brands, or product groups with or without distributor brands.

It seems reasonable to assume that decision making is simpler, if: 1) fewer criteria are used, and 2) the criteria are product specific rather than product related variables, and product related rather than product group variables. If these assumptions are granted, a common pattern evolves, and we can draw the following conclusions: (See Figure 5-2.)

- It is easier to decide on new products (acceptance) than on old products (deletion). (Decision category a versus e and b versus g.) In acceptance decisions, there are no established relations between the product in question and current products, while in deletion decisions there are established relations which can be quite complicated.
- It is easier to make a deletion decision affecting distributor brands than one affecting manufacturer brands. (Decision category f versus e.) The only threat to distributor brands is unsatisfactory sales figures, while the manufacturer brands are deleted for a variety of reasons. In particular, manufacturer brands may be dropped, because they compete too closely with distributor brands, while the contrary does not hold true.
- It is easier to decide on the deletion of manufacturer brands, if there are no distributor brands in the product group. (Decision category c versus d.) The

Decision categories / Characteristics of criteria	Acceptance/rejection of new products		Retention/deletion of old products					Variables not used
	a) Manufacturer brands	b) Both manufacturer and distributor brands	Manufacturer brands			f) Distributor brands	g) Both manufacturer and distributor brands	
			c) Product groups without distributor brands	d) Product groups with distributor brands	e) All product groups			
Product group variables	DISTRIB	-	-	GRPSIZE GRADSIZE	GRPSIZE GRADSIZE DISTRIB	-	GRPSIZE GRADSIZE DISTRIB	GRPSALE
Product related variables	PRICE	PRICE	-	-	-	-	-	SIZE NEWNESS SHARE
Product specific variables	CAMPAIGN	CAMPAIGN	MARKLEAD REGHOUSE STORE	MARKLEAD PRODSALE	PRODSALE	PRODSALE REGHOUSE	PRODSALE REGHOUSE	-
	3	2	3	4	4	2	5	4

Figure 5-2: Characteristics of the Criteria Used in Different Decision Categories

presence of distributor brands makes the product group more important to the decision makers, hence they tend to be more circumspect.

One reason why a decision is perceived as complicated may be its importance to the decision maker. If this is so, the observations mentioned above support the hypothesis, advanced in Section 1.5, that in organizational decision making, there is a concept of involvement analogous to the one operative in consumer buying behavior. In an organizational context, however, importance is more appropriate than involvement. But the relationship is the same: the greater the importance of a decision for the decision maker, the greater the number and complexity of the criteria applied to it. Deletion decisions have more profound consequences than acceptance decisions. (See Section 1.3.) Manufacturer brand decisions may not be more important than distributor brand decisions, but, nevertheless, they are more difficult to make, as the degree of uncertainty is fairly high. When there are distributor brands in a product group, manufacturer brand decisions are certainly more critical for the reseller.

Furthermore, from the presentation of our findings it should be clear that the product and the assortment have other characteristics which affect the importance attributed to different decision criteria. Two examples may be given:

- If the supplier is a market leader, the decision maker will take this into account.
- Which criteria are used is affected by whether the product group is comprised of specialty items or standard products.

Finally, other situational relations can be observed, if the findings are related to the specific characteristics of the enterprise, presented in Section 3.2. Some of these characteristics may be repeated here:

- The enterprise is very large, has a high market share and is vertically integrated to a very high degree.
- It is a union of consumer cooperatives.
- It has a large number of distributor brands, most of them manufactured in its own factories.
- The assortment building function of the organization is highly formalized and routinized.

Against this background, some of the findings can be better understood both with regard to details and in general. The fact that the enterprise is more solicitous about its own brands than most other studies have observed in resellers, is a consequence of its struggle for independence, its consumer cooperative business form and its largescale involvement in manufacturing. The same factors also explain why it sometimes takes a cautious attitude toward market-leading suppliers. The high degree of vertical integration is closely related to the finding that the degree of warehouse coverage is a crucial criterion for deletion decisions. Furthermore, considering the characteristics of the enterprise, it should also be easier to see that the various criteria, taken together, form a consistent pattern.

The enterprise's consumer cooperative business form thus has an indirect effect on the assortment building, i.e, it is a strategic factor. On the other hand, the consumer interest goal, implied in this business form, is hardly apparent in the specific findings of the study, which relate to the tactical level. Indeed, the general pattern of findings indicates that profitability is the goal that guides assortment decision making: supplier marketing campaigns are decisive for addition decisions, the price variable has no effect in deletion cases, etc. This supports the hypothesis, advanced in Section 3.3, that KF has deteriorated, viewed from the cooperative perspective; this is especially true of the assortment building function, which has a strongly commercial orientation.

Nevertheless, on the basis of the conclusions reached in the previous study of KF, we are of the opinion that consumer interest factors are actually somewhat more important than the present study is able to convey. The research is based on the organization's product fact sheets, which mainly contain objective data. Consumer interest aspects are predominantly of a subjective nature, hence, they are most often conveyed through the information sources not included in the study. The data in the product fact sheets most closely approaching the consumer interest dimension are the consumer panel test results, but these are, as already mentioned, unsuited for use in the present study.

This discussion of our specific findings should make it clear that we consider it inadvisable to transfer their validity to other enterprises, other countries, other periods of time etc. - just as inadvisable as generalizing from other studies of reseller assortment building criteria. The situational factors have proved to be very important, hence, a contingency approach is always wise when dealing with such criteria. The suggestion may be useful to other researchers in this field and to its practitioners, whether manufacturers or resellers.

While the salience of situational factors argues for the importance of the contingency approach and moves us to caution against generalizing from our specific findings, we do not hesitate to emphasize the general validity and usefulness of our basic methodological approach, viz., seeking out systematic patterns in decision criteria, as opposed to merely identifying the criteria. Indeed, we consider this as the principal theme and main contribution of the present study. It has been shown that such patterns can be statistically detected and logically explained, given a proper understanding especially of contingent background factors.

APPENDIX A
Statistical Binary-Choice Models

In a binary choice model the response variable Y takes on only the values 0 and 1. If $\mathbf{x}' = (1,x_1,x_2,...,x_p)$ is a given value of the predictor variable vector $\mathbf{X}' = (1,X_1,X_2,..X_p)$ and $\mathbf{\beta}' = (\beta_0,\beta_1,\beta_2,....,\beta_p)$ a parameter vector, then it is assumed that the probability of Y = 1 is a function F of the linear combination $\mathbf{x}'\mathbf{\beta} = \beta_0 + \beta_1 x_1 + \beta_2 x_2 + ... + \beta_p x_p$, that is

$$P(Y = 1) = F(\mathbf{x}'\mathbf{\beta}) \tag{A.1}$$

Consequently, it is assumed that $P(Y=0)=1-F(\mathbf{x}'\mathbf{\beta})$.

The application of the linear specification of the predictor variables makes it possible to use existing computer packages. It is however possible to make non-linear transformations of the predictor variables before the application of the linear specification.

It is now assumed that Y for a given value of the predictor variable $\mathbf{X} = \mathbf{x}$ is Bernouilli-distributed with paramter $P(Y = 1) = P$, where $P = F(\mathbf{x}'\mathbf{\beta})$.

The probability function of Y is then given by

$$P(Y=y) = P^y (1-P)^{1-y} \qquad y=0,1 \tag{A.2a}$$

or

$$P(Y=y) = [F(\mathbf{x}'\mathbf{\beta})]^y[1-F(\mathbf{x}'\mathbf{\beta})]^{1-y} \qquad y=0,1. \tag{A.2b}$$

The expected value of the Bernouilli variable Y is E(Y) = P, and from the binary choice model it follows that

$$E(Y) = F(\mathbf{x}'\mathbf{\beta}) = F(\beta_0 + \beta_1 x_1 + \beta_2 x_2 + ... + \beta_p x_p) \tag{A.3}$$

The variance of Y Var(Y) is found to be

$$Var(Y) = P(1-P) = F(\mathbf{x}'\mathbf{\beta})[1-F(\mathbf{x}'\mathbf{\beta})] \tag{A.4}$$

As $P = F(\mathbf{x}'\mathbf{\beta})$ is a probability, then the function F is restricted to the interval [0,1], that is

$$0 \leqslant F(\mathbf{x}'\mathbf{\beta}) \leqslant 1 \quad \text{for} \quad -\infty < \mathbf{x}'\mathbf{\beta} < \infty$$

Now let $z = \mathbf{x}'\mathbf{\beta}$, then $P = F(z)$ is interpreted as the distribution function of the stochastic variable $Z = \mathbf{X}'\mathbf{\beta}$, that is $P = F(z) = P(Z \leqslant z)$.

The regression version of the model (A.3) can be stated as

$$Y_j = F(\mathbf{x}_j'\mathbf{\beta}) + \varepsilon_j \quad j=1,2,...,n \qquad (A.5)$$

where j is the observation number and ε_j the error term.

We will now present two different probability models, that is, two different specifications of the function F. These are

1. the uniform distribution function (the linear probability model) (LP)
2. the logistic distribution function (the logit model).

As will be seen later, the LP model results in the application of linear regression analysis and the logit model in logistic regression analysis.

The linear probability model
The most simple functional form of F is the identical function, that is, $F(\mathbf{x}'\mathbf{\beta}) = \mathbf{x}'\mathbf{\beta}$, and the regression form (A.5) reduces to

$$Y_j = \mathbf{x}_j'\mathbf{\beta} + \varepsilon_j$$
$$= \beta_0 + \beta_1 x_{1j} + \beta_2 x_{2j} + ... + \beta_p x_{pj} + \varepsilon_j \quad j=1,2,...,n \qquad (A.6)$$

This is the linear probability model, and the interpretation of this model is simple: the probability of $Y_j = 1$ is a linear function of all the predictor variables, and when variable x_k is increased by Δx_k, given that the other predictors are unchanged, then the probability changes with the amount $\beta_k \Delta x_k$.

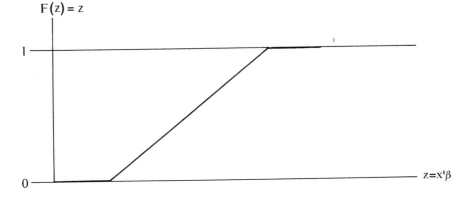

The figure shows the distribution function of statistical variable $Z = \mathbf{X'B}$, which is uniformly distributed on the interval $[0,1]$. It can be seen that the LP-model must satisfy the condition

$$P_j = \begin{cases} 0 & \text{for } \mathbf{x'_j B} < 0 \\ \mathbf{x'B} & \text{for } 0 \leqslant \mathbf{x'_j B} \leqslant 1 \\ 1 & \text{for } \mathbf{x'_j B} > 1 \end{cases} \qquad (A.7)$$

The figure above and equation (A.7) clearly show an obvious drawback of the LP Model: if $\mathbf{x'_j B} < 0$, then the observation will always belong to the category $y = 0$, and if $\mathbf{x_j'B} > 1$, the category will always be $y = 1$. This is a rather unrealistic assumption.

We get the same problem in relation to the estimated probabilities $\hat{P}_j \approx P_j$. Let **b** be the estimate of $\mathbf{B}$, then

$$\hat{P}_j = \begin{cases} 0 & \text{for } \mathbf{x'_j b} < 0 \\ \mathbf{x'_j b} & \text{for } 0 \leqslant \mathbf{x'_j b} \leqslant 1 \\ 1 & \text{for } \mathbf{x'_j b} > 1 \end{cases} \qquad (A.8)$$

Besides the unrealistic kinks of the F-function, the regression model (A.5) is heteroscedastic, because $\text{Var}(\varepsilon_j) = \text{Var}(Y_j) = P_j(1-P_j)$, so ordinary least square (OLS) is not an efficient estimation method. The estimates of $\mathbf{B}$'s are, however, both unbiased and consistent. Weighted least squares (WLS) will produce asymptotically more efficient estimates than OLS (if $0 < \mathbf{x'B} < 1$ is satisfied), but WLS fails if the condition is not met. Furthermore, WLS is quite sensitive to errors of specification; so if the LP-model is used, it will only be in the preliminary stages of the study and only in the OLS-version thanks to its very low costs of computing the estimates. (Amemiya 1981, Pindyck & Rubinfeld, 1981).

It is also possible to use two group discriminant analysis, because this is in principle the same as OLS regression analysis when the response variable is dichotomous. In both analyses the objective is to find a linear combination $Z = \mathbf{x'b}$ of the predictor variables: in regression analysis, so that the correlation between Y and Z is maximum; in discriminant analysis, so that the variation between the two group means $\bar{Z}_0$ and $\bar{Z}_1$ relative to the within group variation is maximum. It can be shown that the two criteria lead to the same linear combination $Z = \mathbf{x'b}$, although the coefficients in the discriminant function are only determined up to multiplication by a constant.

The logit model
In order to avoid the theoretical problems of the LP-model, we introduce the logistic distribution function $L(z) = 1/(1+e^{-z})$ in equation (A.1) and get

$$P(Y=1) = P = L(\mathbf{x'\beta}) = \frac{1}{1+e^{-\mathbf{x'\beta}}} \qquad (A.9)$$

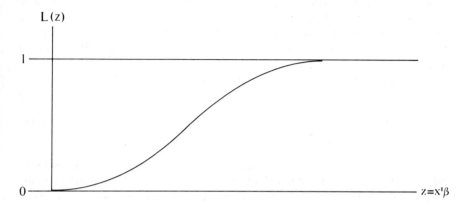

In this figure the shape of the logistic distribution function is shown. It is quite similar to that of the normal distribution, but mathematically more simple. This is because $L(\mathbf{x'\beta})$ is given an explicitly functional form (A.9), while the normal distribution function $\Phi(\mathbf{x'\beta})$ can only be represented by an integral,

$$\Phi(\mathbf{x'\beta}) = \int_{-\infty}^{\mathbf{x'\beta}} \frac{1}{\sqrt{2\pi}} e^{-\frac{u^2}{2}} \, du$$

The relative simplicity of the logistic distribution function makes it advantageous to use this function.

From the figure above, it is seen that the logistic distribution function does not possess the two unrealistic kinks as the uniform distribution function. The problem of probabilities equal to 0 or 1 when $\mathbf{x'\beta}$ is less than 0 or greater than 1, respectively, does not exist here. $L(\mathbf{x'\beta})$ only converges to 0 or 1 as $\mathbf{x'\beta}$ goes to $-\infty$ or $+\infty$, respectively.

In order to make an interpretation of the ß-coefficient, it is convenient to reformulate the model (A.9) into

$$\text{logit } P = \log \frac{P}{1-P} = \mathbf{x'\beta} \qquad (A.10)$$

which says that the logit transformation of P is a linear function $\mathbf{x'\beta}$ of the predictor variables, $\mathbf{x}$.

For continuous predictor variables x_k, the following can be shown: when x_k is increased by Δx_k, then the probability P is approximately increased by $\beta_k P(1-P)\Delta x_k$. This means, that the change in P depends on both the size (and the sign) of β_k and on the size of P itself. It also follows that the sensitivity of P to changes in x_k is maximum, when P is in the proximity of $1/2$.

If the predictor variable x_k is discrete or even dichotomous, it is still valid to say that a positive (negative) sign of β_k combined with an increase in x_k is consistent with an increase (decrease) in P. The sensitivity of P to change in x_k is still greater for moderate P (close to $1/2$) than for extreme P (close to 0 or 1).

The regression version of the logit model (A.10) is given by

$$Y_j = L(x_j'\beta) + \varepsilon_j = \frac{1}{1+e^{-x_j'\beta}} + \varepsilon_j \quad j=1,2,...,n \qquad (A.11)$$

When estimating the coefficient vector β, we use the maximum likelihood estimation method. This method produces estimates with the most superior properties, including efficiency, sufficiency, consistency and asymptotical normality. The likelihood function LF can be found by combining equations (A.2) and (A.9):

$$LF = \prod_{j=1}^{n} P_j^{y_j} \; (1-P_j)^{1-y_j} \qquad (A.12)$$

where $P_j = L(x_j'\beta) = \dfrac{1}{1+e^{-x_j'\beta}}$

The log likelihood function $1 = \ln LF$ is given by

$$1 = \sum_{j=1}^{n} y_j \log P_j + \sum_{j=1}^{n} (1-y_j)\log (1-P_j)$$

$$\qquad (A.13)$$

$$= \sum_{j=1}^{n} y_j \log \frac{P_j}{1-P_j} + \sum_{j=1}^{n} \log(1-P_j)$$

$$= \sum_{j=1}^{n} y_j \, x_j'\beta - \sum_{j=1}^{n} \log(1+e^{x_j'\beta})$$

The maximum likelihood estimates $\hat{\beta}' = (\beta_0, \beta_1, ..., \beta_p)$ is the value of β' that maximizes the LF-function in (A.12) or the 1-function in (A.13).

Differentiating 1 with respect to β_i, $i=0,1,...,p$, we get the p+1 likelihood equations:

$$\sum_{j=1}^{n} (y_j-\hat{P}_j) = 0$$

$$\sum_{j=1}^{n} x_{1j}(y_j - \hat{P}_j) = 0 \qquad\qquad\qquad (A.14a)$$

$$\vdots$$

$$\sum_{j=1}^{n} x_{pj}(y_j - \hat{P}_j) = 0$$

or

$$\sum_{j=1}^{n} x_j(y_j - \hat{P}_j) = 0 \qquad\qquad\qquad (A.14b)$$

where $\hat{P}_j = L(x_j'\hat{\beta}) = \dfrac{1}{1+e^{-x_j'\hat{\beta}}}$

From the first equation in (A.14a) it follows that the predicted frequency of $y = 1$ is equal to the actual frequency of $y = 1$. And if a predictor variable say x_1 is a dummy, then it follows that the predicted and the actual frequency of $y = 1$ will be equal for each of the subsamples defined by $x_1 = 1$ and $x_1 = 0$. (Maddala 1983).

Since the likelihood equations (A.14) are non-linear in $\hat{\beta}$, the estimate of β must be computed by an interative method. We use the computer program PLR (logistic regression) based on the iterative Newton-Raphson method from the computer package BMDP Statistical Software. (Engelman 1981).

Although the costs of computing the ML-estimates of the logit model are greater than the costs of computing the least squares estimates of the LP-model, we prefer the logit model due to the more satisfying theoretical and statistical properties of this model.

APPENDIX B
Studies in Reseller Assortment Decision Criteria

This appendix contains short synopses of 34 previous studies of reseller assortment decision criteria. It purposes to give a comprehensive survey of previous research within this subject area, but no doubt the list is not entirely exhaustive. Nevertheless, we believe no major work has eluded our attention.

The essential element in this presentation is the criteria which the various studies have observed. To provide a basis for understanding the character of the studies, we also state, when possible, the object of study (country, industry, distribution channel level, type of assortment decisions), their method (data collection and compilation, literature base), and their scientific intent (scope,

Authors	Country	Industry	Channel Level	Decision Type	Basis
Nigut 1958	USA	Grocery	Wholesale	New	Empirical
Gordon 1961	USA	Grocery	Wholesale	New	?
Hileman & Rosenstein 1961	USA	Grocery	Wholesale	New	Empirical
Kihlstedt 1961	Sweden	Various	Retail	New	Empirical
McNeill 1962	USA	Textiles	Retail	New	Empirical
Food Trade Marketing Council 1964a	USA	Grocery	Wholesale	New	Empirical
Food Trade Marketing Council 1964b	USA	Grocery	Wholesale	New	Empirical
Einstein 1965	USA	?	?	New	?
Borden 1968	USA	Grocery	Wholesale	New/Old	Empirical
Graf 1968	USA	Grocery	Wholesale	New	Empirical
Grashof 1968	USA	Grocery	Wholesale	New/Old	Empirical
Berens 1969	USA	Men's wear	Retail	New	Empirical
Lebensmittel-Zeitung 1970	Germany	Grocery	Retail	New	Empirical
Hix 1972	USA	Men's wear	Retail	New	Empirical
Doyle & Weinberg 1973	UK	Grocery	Wholesale	New	Empirical
Heeler et al 1973	Canada	Grocery	Wholesale	New	Empirical
Coops & Voluntaries 1974	USA	Grocery	?	New	?
Sweitzer 1974	USA	Grocery	Wholesale	New	Empirical
Arora 1975	USA	Grocery	Wholesale	New	Empirical
Davidson et al 1975	USA	Various	?	New	?
Gripsrud & Olsen 1975	Norway	Grocery	Wholesale	New	Empirical
Hutt 1975	USA	Grocery	Wholesale	New	Empirical
Kaiser 1975	Germany	Grocery	Wholesale	New	Empirical
Lebensmittel-Zeitung 1975	Germany	Grocery	Wholesale	New	Empirical
Montgomery 1975	USA	Grocery	Wholesale	New	Empirical
Johnson 1976	UK	Grocery	Wholesale	New	Empirical
Lindqvist 1976	Finland	Grocery	Wholesale	New	Empirical
Progressive Grocer 1978	USA	Various	Wholesale	New	Empirical
Bauer 1980	Germany	Grocery	Various	New	Literature
Douglas 1980	UK	Grocery	Wholesale	New	Empirical
Nilsson 1980	Sweden	Grocery	Wholesale	New/Old	Empirical
Sauer 1982	Germany	Grocery	Retail	New	Empirical
Swinnen 1983	Belgium	Grocery	Retail	New/Old	Empirical
Angelmar & Pras 1984	USA/France	Movies	Import	New	Empirical

Figure B-1: Characteristics of 34 Studies on Reseller Assortment Decision Criteria

aim, vested interest). Some of these characteristics are summarized in Figure B-1.

NIGUT conducted a survey among executives in fifty large US supermarket chains in order to identify their buying criteria. (Nigut 1958, pp. 11-12.) The survey resulted in the following ranking of criteria:

1. Will it return a fair dollar profit in terms of the potential volume and the shelf space it will occupy?
2. Does the consumer want it?
3. What is its sales potential?
4. Is there really a need for the product?
5. How will the product be advertised and promoted?
6. Are there advertising, promotional and/or display allowances available?
7. Is there a retailer incentive?
8. Is the product of good quality?
9. Is it properly and sensibly packaged?
10. Is the manufacturer reliable?
11. Does competition have this item?
12. Was the product market tested?
13. Is the product timely - in season?
14. Is the introduction timely?
15. Will it help bringing new customer traffic to our stores?
16. How is the product packed?
17. Does stocking the item conflict with existing company policy?

In another article, 14 years later, Nigut published the same list of criteria, but with the addition of an eighteenth criterion: "Does the product contribute to the pollution of our air and water?" (Nigut 1972, p. 60.)

In a review of buying committees in supermarket chains, GORDON wrote: (Gordon 1961, p. 59.)

Of all the items accepted by buying committees, practically three-quarters of them are added to the store shelves for *greater selection, sales,* and *profits.* Other important reasons for adding are *consumer demand, manufacturer's action,* such as changes in size, label, promotion and *"stocked by major competition".* The buying committee's largest single reason for discontinuing items is insufficient volume and profit. *"Slow movement"* of items accounts for almost half of the discontinued products. Items are also dropped if they have not fulfilled expectations, or they may even be replaced by superior quality products. (Emphasis added.)

Regrettably, Gordon failed to mention what basis he had for these statements.

HILEMAN and ROSENSTEIN attended and tape-recorded a buying committee meeting in a grocery chain. They identified no less than 58 factors that the committee considered when deciding on new product additions. These were classified in seven categories: Product characteristics (8 factors), Packaging (6), Miscellaneous factors (15), Merchandising (10), Advertising (8), Profit area (9) and Competitive aspects (2). They summarized their impressions as follows: (Hileman & Rosenstein 1961, p. 55.)

In general, at this buying session certain factors appeared each time a product adoption occured. Basically, there was an element of *newness* - of something different. The item did *not duplicate* in type, size or price an item already carried in the stores. The presence of a "gimmick" or something a little extra in the way of packaging helped. And the existence of supporting advertising, not only in *introducing* the product but in *continual promotion* carried a great deal of weight in influencing favorable decision. (Emphasis added.)

KIHLSTEDT conducted a study of retail assortment policy in ten product categories in four industries in Sweden: groceries, chemical dye and drugs, hardware and clothing. He found that purchases co-varied with the retailers' evaluations of various factors, in the following order (arithmetic means of rank correlation coefficients): (Kihlstedt 1961, pp. 168-171. Our translation.)

1. Supplier assortment (depth) (0.41)
2. Supplier representatives (0.35)
3. Supplier price differentiation system (discount policy) (0.34)
4. Supplier credit terms (0.31)
5. Supplier price level (0.27)
6. Supplier quality level (0.27)
7. Supplier delivery systems (0.26)
8. Supplier advertising and promotion (0.11)

The following new product selection criteria were "developed by MCNEILL after observing and discussing the procurement of several items with a buyer of draperies and upholsteries:" (McNeill 1962, quoted from Hix 1972, pp. 14-16.)

- Compatability with or ability to modify to fit present merchandise line
- Availability of current sales
- Familiarity of resource
- Availability from established source
- Price
- Advertising support
- Volume generating ability (without advertising)
- Cost and mark-up
- Existing open-to-buy
- Substitutability of current order and ability to cancel existing order
- Alternative uses of funds

In a report, published in 1964 by the FOOD TRADE MARKETING COUNCIL, the following list of new product buying criteria is reported to be applied by food chains. (The Food Trade Marketing Council 1964 (a), p. 16, cited from Davidson, Doody & Sweeney 1975, p. 335.) The criteria are ranked in order of descending importance.

1. Usefulness of product
2. Does not duplicate an existing item
3. Product profitability
4. Advertising support
5. Gross margin
6. Appearance of package
7. Quality of package
8. Retail price
9. Good experience with manufacturer's other products
10. Reputation of supplier
11. Test market results
12. Introductory allowance
13. Advertising allowance
14. Amount of shelf space occupied
15. Deals offered
16. In-store merchandising support
17. Competitor's action on new item
18. Item well presented by salesman

From another source, also published by the FOOD TRADE MARKETING COUNCIL in 1964, we find some other findings. The following list presents the ten most influential factors mentioned by food distributors in decisions to stock or not to stock a new item: (The Food Trade Marketing Council 1964 (b), p. 26, cited from Grashof 1968, p. 29.)

1. Proven demand for the product
2. Adequate advertising and promotion support
3. Proof that competition is successfully moving item
4. Free merchandise with purchase
5. Advertising allowance
6. Display allowance
7. Case pack commensurate with anticipated movement
8. Cash discount
9. Does not require excessive amount of display space
10. Other

According to Hix, EINSTEIN "suggests a list of criteria important in the selection of a new item. The questions he says a buyer can ask himself in considering a new item are:" (Einstein 1965, p. 277, cited from Hix 1972, pp. 16-17.)

1. Does the article fit in with the character of the store and the department?
2. Is it attractively priced? An article may be well worth the money the store would have to charge for it, but is that price attractive to the store's own customers?

3. Does it offer sufficient markon to produce a profit? If not, the effort to launch it may be love's labor lost.
4. Is it likely to become a volume item? If not, does it have a prestige value?
5. Is it a conversation piece and does it bring interest to the department?
6. Will it perform satisfactorily? Perhaps it has been, or can be, laboratory tested. If it is mechanical or electrical, it must qualify for approval by recognized authorities or agencies.
7. Has it been wear-tested or use-tested? Have you tried it yourself to be sure that it will do the things it should, and as represented?
8. Has it been sold elsewhere? With what results and by what methods?
9. What might its effects be on similar items in stock?

BORDEN followed five new products on their way through the decision-making process in 27 large US supermarket chains. His method was observation of and interviews with salesmen, buyers and buying committees. The results of the study comprise descriptions of the decision process and explanations of the importance of various influential factors, among them the buying criteria.

Borden's findings regarding buying criteria are quite interesting, though they deviate remarkably from what other researchers report:

At the outset of this study it was expected that it would be possible to ascertain the criteria or standards used by the trade to judge the adequacy of the various elements of the product proposition. Unfortunately, such specific buying criteria could not be developed primarily because (1) supermarket firms themselves did not appear to have any specifically defined criteria, and (2) trade evaluations (particularly in buying committees) were too brief, unstructured, often superficial, and varying among firms to permit a determination of specific criteria on the basis of observed behavior. (Borden 1968, p. 202.)

In the absence of specific, defined criteria, were there perhaps more general criteria implicit in the buying behavior? Using a fairly broad definition of criteria, there did appear to be some common measures or questions applied by the trade to the five products. These were:

(1) Did the item "look like it would sell?"
(2) Was the manufacturer going to advertise and promote the product strongly enough to make acceptance desirable or necessary?
(3) Were the "deal" terms (primarily margin and allowance) in line with the category and experience with the manufacturer?

While these criteria might impress the reader as being too shallow and general to reflect considered buying, they are, in the writer's opinion, practically all that can be justified by observing buying behavior. It should be pointed out, however, that had the research been designed to go much beyond observed behavior as the basis for imputing buying criteria, it is quite possible that more refined and additional criteria (normally unwritten and unspoken) might have come to light. (Borden 1968, pp. 202-203.)

GRAF investigated how buyers in 14 supermarket chains evaluate various elements in the supplier representatives' new product presentations. (Graf 1968, pp. 68-69.) More specifically, Graf asked the buyer to assess the importance of 45 elements of information within five categories on a scale from zero to three. The findings were as follows:

1. The advertising/promotion program: 2.7
    1 a) Pack offer (3.0)
    1 b) Sampling at head-quarters (2.8)
    1 c) Spot TV (2.7)
    1 d) Magazine/newspaper advertising (2.7)
    1 e) Couponing (2.6)
    1 f) Network TV (2.3)

2. The item description: 2.5
    2 a) Ingredients (3.0)
    2 b) Cost (2.7)
    2 c) Suggested retail (2.5)
    2 d) Name (2.4)
    2 e) Container type (2.4)
    2 f) Margin (2.4)
    2 g) When available (2.3)
    2 h) Suggested order size (2.3)
    2 i) Palletized (2.3)
    2 j) Contents (2.1)
    2 k) Case pack (2.0)
    2 l) Container shape (1.9)
    2 m) Federal regulations (1.8)

3. Evidence of consumer acceptance rates as established by tests: 2.3
    3 a) Store tested (2.7)
    3 b) Test marketed (2.5)
    3 c) Marketing program in test (2.5)
    3 d) In-store promotion (2.5)
    3 e) Results of test (2.4)
    3 f) Demand by demographics (2.4)
    3 g) Other promotion (2.4)
    3 h) Anticipated demand (2.3)
    3 i) Length of test (1.6)

4. The detailing of introductory terms and allowances: 2.3
    4 a) Samples for store (3.0)
    4 b) Other (2.7)
    4 c) Advance allowance (2.6)
    4 d) Display allowance (2.5)
    4 e) Discount (2.5)
    4 f) How paid (2.5)

    4 g) Guaranteed sale (2.4)
    4 h) Samples for head-quarters (2.3)
    4 i) Length of time (2.1)
    4 j) Store coverage (2.0)
    4 k) Trade advertising (2.0)
    4 l) Display material (1.6)

5. The presentation of the reasons for the item development: 1.4
    5 a) To meet consumer needs (1.9)
    5 b) To increase overall sales (1.6)
    5 c) Product improvement (1.3)
    5 d) To fill out the line (0.9)
    5 e) Package improvement (0.8)

In another report from the same year, Graf, together with Mueller, present a different version of the above-mentioned factors. The differences are, however, so small that there is reason to assume that they are based on the same study, conducted by A. C. Nielsen Company, and that they only represent different computation methods. According to this report, the importance of the elements, measured on a scale from zero to three is as follows: (Mueller & Graf 1968, pp. 2 and 5.)

Evidence of consumer acceptance	2.5
Advertising / promotion	2.2
Introductory terms and allowances	2.0
Why item was developed	1.9
Merchandising recommendations	1.8

GRASHOF studied the assortment building process of supermarkets, using two very different methodologies. (Grashof 1968 and 1970.) To begin with, he conducted case studies on five large supermarkets chains, conducting in-depth interviews with buying managers, buyers and data-processing personnel, and attending buying-committee meetings and salesman presentations. Then, based on the findings of the case studies, Grashof conducted three simulation experiments, one representing the work flow of the buying department, the other the process of evaluating the products and the third the allocation of the store's shelf space. Grashof's study is of special interest, as it differs from most other studies in several crucial respects:

- The product mix decisions were considered to be of two kinds: addition and delation decisions, and both were analysed.
- Grashof discussed the interplay between addition and delation decisions, and likewise, he laid great stress on the relations between the product under consideration and the total product mix.
- Grashof did not regard the various decision criteria as a mechanically

compiled list, but treated them as a system, where there are many complex ties between the criteria.
- Profitability was regarded as the ultimate goal for the chain, and hence, all criteria are subordinate to this profitability goal.

Based on a literature survey, Grashof compiled the following list of 14 product-mix decision criteria: (Grashof 1968, p. 6.)

- Estimate of sales volume
- The supplier's promotional program
- Test market data
- Unit cost
- Unit retail
- Unit size
- Gross margin
- Promotional data
- Introductory allowances
- Sales of competing items
- Gross margin dollars generated per unit time
- Newness
- Reactions of competitors to the item
- Effect on product mix of addition or deletion

According to Grashof's findings from the case studies, the chains' decision criteria for addition decisions are: (Grashof 1968, pp. 68-72.)

There is little question that the most important criteria in all chains is demonstrated consumer demand for an item. ... However, only rarely, if ever, can the salesman prove consumer demand for his item ... Therefore, in most instances, the item offered is evaluated on the basis of two other general considerations.

1: The first general consideration is an attempt to apply the consumer demand criteria mentioned above ... Since the chain can not know beforehand what the demand is going to be, several other criteria are used; criteria that are supposed to be indicative of consumer demand.

   1a: The first and foremost of the secondary criteria is the promotional program of the supplier ... a large, expensive promotional program ... a strong national advertising program ... couponing and/or sampling is to be conducted in the chain's local market ... Guaranteed advertising programs.

   1b: A second factor evaluated as part of the estimate of consumer demand for the new item is test market data.

   1c: The third factor used by chains to estimate consumer demand for a new item is the sales history of competing items ... Particular attention is given to trends in the sale of the product family and to shifts in sales patterns within the product family.

1d: The fourth factor affecting a chain's estimate of the consumer demand for a new item is the attitude of competition as reflected by the competitive chains that have added the item to their product lines.

2:   The second general consideration chains use in evaluating new items is the effect of the item on the mix of items carried by the chains ... ... The factors considered when chains evaluate an item under the general consideration of product mix are:
   1)   Unit cost.
   2)   Unit retail.
   3)   Unit size.
   4)   Number of items with which it competes.
   5)   Similarities with competing items.
   6)   Differences with competing items.
   7)   Sales of competing items.

3:   There are several other factors, in addition to the above, which chains consider when evaluating a new item.
   3a: One of the factors is the reputations of the firm offering the product. The chains consider the dependability and reliability of the firm with respect to service, and also consider the firm's reputations for ethical business dealings and successful introduction of new items.
   3b: A second factor considered is the gross margin per cent that the manufacturer suggests.
   3c: Third on the list of specific factors considered in evaluating new item offerings are the introductory deals and the promotional allowances available.
   3d: A fourth factor considered is the quality of the product's handling characteristics.
   3e: Closely related to the aspect of physical handling characteristics are freight allowances and/or back haul privileges.

As for deletion decisions, Grashof stated: (Grashof 1968, pp. 78-79.)

The prime factor in the identification of items for possible deletion, as well as the most important criterion used in the decision is lack of demonstrated consumer demand for an item as indicated by a low rate of sales for the item.

Another important criterion is the level of the gross margin of the item .... especially when compared with other items in the same product family .....

The two factors mentioned above can be combined to provide a third criterion - gross margin dollars generated per unit time.

For all three of the above criteria many chains consider the trend more important than the absolute level at any point of time.

A fourth criterion ....The chains, in their desire to maintain variety on the store's shelves, will hesitate to delete one-of-a-kind items.

Occasionally an item might be dropped due to a need for shelf space in its product category.

Summarizing his findings, Grashof wrote: (Grashof 1968, Abstract.)

The results of the case study showed the most widely used criteria for product mix decisions to be:

1) Movement
2) The promotional program of the supplier
3) The gross margin per cent of the item
4) The introductory program (for new items)
5) The newness of the item (for new items)
6) The role of the item in the total mix og items carried by the chain.

BERENS conducted a study of the assortment building process in a small independent men's wear store. (Berens 1969 and 1971-1972.) He constructed a logical-flow model of the decision process and tested this with the help of a simulation technique. Among the variables in the model were decision criteria. Based on literature surveys and observations of and interviews with retailers, Berens identified 29 choice criteria.

The findings show that there is considerable variance in what criteria are applied. Firstly, the two buyers of the men's wear store made somewhat different evaluations. Berens explained this by referring to the fact that the two buyers had quite different professional backgrounds. (Berens 1969, p. 20.) Secondly, the importance of the criteria varied with the product category, such as clothing, sportswear and furnishings. Thirdly, Berens tested the results obtained from the study of the two buyers on a sample of 26 other men's wear stores in the same region, and he found that these differed considerably from the pattern of the first store. These differences in assortment choice criteria were, Berens claimed, due to differences in the business policy of the stores. While the store being studied was modern and fashion-conscious, the 26 other stores had conservative managements. (Berens 1969, p. 126.)

The assortment choice criteria which Berens identified were: (Berens 1969, pp. 161-164.)

- Supplier offers advertising allowances
- Supplier offers point of purchase promotional material
- Supplier offers good credit terms
- Supplier assists firm in inventory control
- Supplier sells and promotes a "name" line
- Supplier is reliable in fulfilling promises made.
- Mark-up is adequate
- Transportation costs are reasonable
- Supplier has a stock service
- We will be the only one ... carrying the item
- Expected turnover of supplier's line is at least 4 times a year
- Items in the line will promote the sale of other items
- Expected customer return of complaint rate satisfactory.

- Suppliers' packaging is adequate
- Others in the store like the line
- Supplier offers incentives to salespeople
- Supplier permits return of unwanted goods
- Supplier's line has significant changes from season to season
- Customers ask for the line
- Opportunity for greater than 40% mark-up exists
- Supplier's line is cut to fit customers well
- Supplier's line is found in stores similar to the store we operate
- Supplier's line contributes to fashion leadership image
- Supplier processes orders and reorders promptly
- Supplier advertises line in local media (radio, TV, newspapers)
- Supplier will sell on a private label basis
- Supplier offers "closeouts" for end of season promotion
- Supplier line is not carried by budget centers and discount houses
- Supplier can fill reorders

In 1969, the West-German trade magazine LEBENSMITTEL-ZEITUNG conducted a survey on food retailers' new-product decision criteria. Persons involved in the selection of new products within 414 relatively large food-retailing companies were asked to state which of 26 presented potential decision criteria they considered to be important. The results were as follows: (Lebensmittel-Zeitung 1970, cited from Bauer 1980, p. 288. Our translation.)

		Cited as "Absolutely decisive"
1.	The manufacturer is a well known and solid company	63%
2.	Very advantageous introductory price for the ultimate consumer	63%
3.	There are proofs that the product has real advantages - is of best quality	56%
4.	Relatively low price for the ultimate consumer	54%
5.	The retailer gets a very advantageous margin	53%
6.	There is vigorous TV advertising	51%
7.	Samples are distributed to consumer households	45%
8.	There is already a long-standing and satisfactory business relation to the producer	42%
9.	There is vigorous direct advertising	41%
10.	The article has a very salable package	38%
11.	There is vigorous newspaper advertising	38%
12.	Fixed price	38%
13.	Very advantageous discounts for subsequent, normal sales	36%
14.	Market research proves that the consumer is really interested in the article	36%
15.	There is vigorous advertising in weeklies	32%
16.	The retailer gets very advantageous introductory rebates, especially in the form of free merchandise	31%
17.	The retailer gets very advantageous introductory rebates, especially in the form of cash discounts	30%

18. Test marketing in a regional, limited market has proven
    that the article is successful   28%
19. There is vigorous billboard advertising   24%
20. There are store demonstrations of the item   23%
21. The manufacturer contributes to the retailer's advertising   22%
22. The manufacturer supplies the store with point-of-purchase material   21%
23. A detailed product description is supplied   19%
24. Consumer pricing is optional   19%
25. Introduction over a long period of time   16%
26. Recommended price   15%

HIX studied decision criteria among men's wear buyers in three Southern states in the USA. A sample of buyers was asked to take respond to 55 statements about products and suppliers. The statements were formulated on the basis of published studies, test interviews and personal advice from other researchers. The data set, comprising answers from 320 buyers, was analysed with the use of factor analysis. Fifteen factors turned out to explain 63.5 percent of the variance (Hix 1972, p. 34), but only eight of these were important enough to mention. (Hix 1972, p. 36.) These eight factors, ranked after importance, were: (Hix 1972, p. 63.)

1. Customer satisfaction
2. Availability
3. Profit potential
4. Support
5. Relationship with salesman (and/or source)
6. Security
7. Direct, non-item inducements
8. Interpersonal influences

After this, Hix carried out a similar survey among suppliers, who were asked to identify the criteria they expected the buyers to apply. The findings were in very close agreement with what the buyers themselves had mentioned. (Hix 1972, pp. 65 f.)

Hix concluded his study by constructing a "New Product Evaluation Sheet" for the use of retailers contemplating the purchase of new items. This scheme contains the following factors: (Hix 1972, p. 87.)

I   *Customer satisfaction*
   - Quality of product
   - Stability of line
   - Speed of delivery
   - Speed of adjustment
   - Relationship to present line

II   *Profit potential*
   - Mark-up

- Turnover
- Traffic generating ability
- Financing aid

III   Availability
- Ability of source to deliver quantity ordered (not on allotment)
- Accessibility for merchandise selection
- Mid-season re-orders

IV   Support
- Advertising (P.O.P., Co-op, etc.)
- Trade discounts
- Exclusive selling in territory
- Known brand

V   Relationship with salesman (and/or source)
- Established relationship
- Knowledgeable salesman
- Frequency of sales calls
- Salesman's overall ability

VI   Others
- Others' experience with item
- Trade papers' feature of item
- Small investment required
- Display allowances

DOYLE and WEINBERG developed a method according to which distributors could use a computerized system for their new product selection. The method requires that the distributor has a file where all current items are evaluated according to a number of criteria, and where there are also scores for the profitability of the products. As a new product is offered to the distributor, the buyer evaluates it according to these criteria. Based on these evaluations and the company's file, it is possible to calculate a forecast for the new product's chances of success.

The two researchers tested their method on 60 products, and it proved quite efficient. Through interviews with buyers in large British supermarkets, they identified the following list of eight decision criteria: (Doyle & Weinberg 1973, p. 51.)

- Potential opportunities in relevant product class
- Marketing reputation of the manufacturer
- Price of the brand compared to competitors
- Quality of the brand compared to competitors
- Contribution margin
- Rating of proposed product launch

- Expected volume compared to others in product class
- Potential profitability to the supermarket if launch successful

HEELER, KEARNEY and MEHAFFEY tested three variants of the Fishbein model on new product decisions of a Canadian grocery wholesaler. Their data base consisted of "Product Presentation Sheets" for 67 products. On the sheet, the researchers identified 13 decision criteria, and the sheets supplied them with information about the products' scores for these criteria. Furthermore, the company informed them whether the products were accepted or rejected. Using regression analysis, the researchers showed that the models could represent the decision making very well. The GLS compensatory model (generalized least squares) was the best one. It contained four explanatory variables: supplier advertising, time discount on payables, number of competing items stocked and gross profit percentage. The complete list of decision criteria was as follows: (Heeler, Kearney & Mehaffey 1973, p. 35.)

- Cooperative advertising
- Number of competing chains carrying the product
- Introductory allowance
- Product velocity
- Gross profit percentage
- Percentage discount on payables
- Time of discount on payables
- Volume rebate
- Minimum order requirement
- Supplier advertising
- Point-of-sale material
- Number of competing items stocked
- Retail representatives in the area

Hutt cited an article, published in CO-OPS AND VOLUNTARIES: (Co-ops and Voluntaries 1974, cited from Hutt 1975, pp. 23-24.)

What criteria do buyers use in selecting new products? Listed in order of importance, the research yielded the following criteria: (1) product profitability, (2) usefulness of product, (3) "newness" of item, (4) advertising support, and (5) test market results. Interestingly, when product managers were asked to estimate the criteria they perceive as being important to buyers, the following list emerged: (1) product profitability, (2) gross margin, (3) advertising support, (4) "newness" of item, and (5) test market results.

SWEITZER analyzed the interaction between sellers and buyers, and especially mechanisms of perceptual biases and other distortions in communication. (Sweitzer 1974.) For this purpose, he identified a list of 18 purchasing criteria, applied by retail chain buyers. The criteria were identified through an open-ended enquiry into the attributes of a new product offer being considered by the buyers. The respondents were a sample af buyers from the merchandising department of a large Midwestern food and dry goods retail chain.

Sweitzer was not interested in the relative importance of the decision criteria. Hence, he did not calculate average importance scores, though he published the evaluations of the criteria made by the seven buyers of the chain. This data was analysed by Arora. Likewise, Arora calculated the relative importance of the decision criteria, using some earlier, unpublished data, which Joseph W. Thompson collected from twelve buyers in an Eastern supermarket chain. (Arora 1974, pp. 171 and 173.) In his study, Thompson used Sweitzer's questionnaire, thus providing comparability.

The criteria which Sweitzer identified are shown below. The figures are Arora's calculations of the average importance of the criteria, using Sweitzer's and Thompson's data. In both cases, the buyers rated the criteria on a scale from one to nine.

ARORA studied various aspects of the new-product adoption process in a medium-sized supermarket chain in the Midwest. One aspect was the decision criteria used by the buyers and the buying committee when selecting new products. Arora identified which criteria were used, the relative importance of each criterion and the degree of conformity among buyers. To identify decision criteria, Arora tape-recorded 52 presentations which supplier representatives made to the buyers, as well as buying committee meetings, where 83 new products were decided on. After the tape-recordings had been transcribed, Arora analyzed the dialogues, and a total of 14 criteria were isolated. The buyers were then given an opportunity to comment and supplement the list of criteria. Arora writes: "In view of the methodology used to isolate the new product decision-making criteria, the researcher feels that the list presented .... is a very comprehensive one of those criteria actually used by the buying committee in the selection of new products, and the list should be used in future research." (Arora 1975, pp. 112-113.)

To assess the relative importance of the criteria, the seven buyers of the supermarket chain were asked to evaluate each criterion on a scale from one to nine. Arora also used a complementary measurement, as he asked the buyers to rank the criteria. The results from the two modes of measuring the importance of the criteria are fairly consonant, though there are a few remarkable divergences.

According to the buyers' ranking of the criteria (the second method of measurement), the relative importance of the criteria is as follows, here ranked in descending order of importance: (Arora 1975, pp. 92-94. The calculation of the importance of the criteria is made by us, on the basis of figures which Arora presents on p. 134.)

	Sweitzer's data		Thompson's data	
	rank	average	rank	average
- Case movement of comparable or similar products	6	7.14	1	8.50
- Potential for "trade-up" to larger size and price	16	6.14	17	5.83
- Value to the consumer as seen in the /company/ "actuals"	12	6.57	7	7.20
- Product quality in terms of manufacturer's specifications	14	6.28	13	6.17
- Amount of advertising/promotional dollars spent by the manufacturer	3	7.57	4	7.92
- Length of time required for an order to arrive at the warehouse, i.e., lead time	18	5.14	18	5.45
- Size of advertising and/or display allowances, deals etc., prorated on a yearly basis	10	6.71	6	7.42
- Nature of the billing on deals, i.e., off-invoice rather than bill-back	7	7.00	16	5.83
- Timing of manufacturer's promotion in relation to the distribution of the product, i.e., advertising before distribution	4	7.57	3	8.00
- Seasonality of product sales	11	6.71	8	7.00
- Availability of local stocks	13	6.42	9	7.00
- Potential value to consumer compared to similar items	2	7.85	5	7.75
- Profit potential of the product	1	8.00	2	8.00
- Distribution and case movement of the product by competitors	17	6.00	10	6.83
- Availability of alternative types of promotional deals in relation to competition	8	7.00	14	6.00
- Type of performance requirements associated with promotional deals	5	7.28	11	6.83
- Shelf space requirements	9	6.71	12	6.58
- Type of packaging, i.e., open stock rather than cut cases, case size, etc.	15	6.14	15	5.91

1. *Sales potential of the product:* determined by the case movement of similar products, supplier's information, test market results, intuitive feeling, or by some other method. (2.0)
2. *Over-all potential profit (in dollars) of the product:* includes gross margins, price of the product after deals and/or allowances. (3.9)
3. *Manufacturer/supplier's backing* (amount of reselling; track record): includes advertising and promotion (especially in the local market), evidence of consumer acceptance (such as test market results), sampling, coupons, deals to consumers, and so forth. (4.2)
4. *Introductory terms and allowances:* includes deals, advertising and display allowances, performance requirements, cooperative advertising, extended billings, method of payment of allowances (such as off invoice, bill back and so forth). (4.7)
5. *Potential value to consumer compared to similar products* after allowing for the difference in label (private versus national brand): the customer is generally willing to pay more for the national brand, compared to a private label. (6.7)
6. *Uniqueness of the product:* one of a kind. (8.1)
7. *Manufacturer's coordination of promotion and advertising programs with distribution* on the product. (8.3)
8. *Service from the supplier:* includes follow-up of orders, deliveries, payment of allowances, information on competitive products, information on local markets, store visits, setting up of displays, product quality in terms of specification, and so forth. (8.6)
9. *Seasonality of product sale.* (8.9)
10. *Requests for the product* by the store managers based on customers' requests. (9.1)
11.-12. *Shelf space requirements.* (9.6)
11.-12. *Overall packaging:* includes packaging size, colors, copy, layout, and so forth. Also includes case size and open stock versus cut case. (9.6)
13. *Avoidance of duplication* of products perceived to be very similar to the one carried now. (10.1)
14. *Potential competitive move of manufacturers selling similar products.* (11.3)

Quite interestingly, Arora found no significant difference in the importance ratings of the decision criteria of different buyers. (Arora 1975, p. 114.)

In most textbooks for retail management courses, there is a more or less comprehensive treatment of new-product decision criteria. As an example can be mentioned the book by DAVIDSON, DOODY and SWEENEY. These authors summarize their discussion with the following list of criteria: (Davidson, Doody & Sweeney 1975, p. 382.)

1. *Merchandise suitability.* Whether past sales experience indicates that the goods offered by a particular vendor are in keeping with the wants and needs of the store's customers.

2. *Prices and terms.* Quoted list prices; deductible trade, quantity, and cash discounts; and transportation charges often vary considerably among vendors. Also to be considered are differences in credit terms, which influence many merchants, particularly those with limited capital resources.
3. *Delivery dates.* Selection of a source of supply often depends upon the length of time required for delivery of wanted merchandise.
4. *Vendor's distribution policy.* If a vendor offers a merchant exclusive representation or if he carefully selects only a limited number of outlets, he usually becomes a preferred resource among the dealers so selected.
5. *Promotional assistance.* Resources that furnish advertising and display material or make available advertising allowances are often selected in preference to those who do not offer such aids.
6. *Reliability.* A vendor's reputation for conforming with promised delivery dates, shipping merchandise that checks with samples, and handling complaints fairly and promptly are important considerations.

GRIPSRUD and OLSEN conducted a number of informal interviews within the four largest chains in the Norwegian grocery trade. Part of the project consisted in studying the assortment building function. Among the findings, mainly the following three propositions concern the assortment decision criteria:

- Large, well known and reliable suppliers have considerably better chances of having their new products accepted. One of the resellers has even made a classification of all potential suppliers, and those in the highest-ranking class have their new products accepted automatically. (Gripsrud & Olsen 1974, pp. 14, 31 and 50.)
- The resellers make great efforts to keep the assortment as well as the number of suppliers limited. Hence, they use the principle of "one in, one out." (Gripsrud & Olsen 1975, pp. 14, 50-51 and 68-69.)
- The reseller's own brands are given high priority. (Gripsrud & Olsen 1975, pp. 33 and 69.)

HUTT investigated the way buying committees work in the grocery trade. (Hutt 1975 and 1979.) More specifically, he analysed the relationships between the structural characteristics of the committees, especially group cohesiveness and leadership, and various characteristics of the decision process, among them, the decision criteria. He also wished to explore whether the decision process is influenced by the type of decision, and above all, by the newness of the product. The study was based on well-structured interviews with a total of 120 members on 22 buying committees representing food retail chains of different organizational setup and located in different metropolitan areas in two Midwestern states.

Based on trade literature and test interviews, Hutt identified seven decision criteria. (Hutt 1975, p. 61.) The buying committee members were asked to assess the importance of the criteria on a scale from one to seven. The average evaluation of the relative importance of the criteria resulted in the following ranking: (The calculation of averages and the ranking are made by us, based on data in Hutt 1975, p. 130.)

1. Reputation of manufacturer	5.78
2. Advertising support	5.68
3. Product "newness"	4.86
4. Introductory deal (e.g., cash off invoice)	3.83
5. Test market results	3.74
6. Introductory advertising allowances	2.31
7. Quality and appearance of package	2.07

Bauer presents some unpublished results from a study conducted by A. KAISER in West Germany in 1975. Kaiser "asked 29 manufacturers (food manufacturers represented the largest group in the sample, but it also contained two suppliers of services) their opinion of the decision criteria used by the trade in adopting new products. Surprisingly, the criteria and their ranking, based on frequency of mention, correspond, by and large, to the criteria and ranking claimed by the decision makers of the trade." (Bauer 1980, pp. 293-294. Our translation. Kaiser's study from 1975 is not published.)

	Times mentioned	
	Number	Frequency
1. The product's advantages satisfy new needs	14	19.2%
2. Sales promotion measured during and after introduction	10	13.7%
3. Margin and discounts	9	12.3%
4. Price conception	7	9.6%
5. Supplying service & sales force	6	8.2%
6. Increased supplies at enduring demand	6	8.2%
7. Image of producer	5	6.9%
8. Experience with other products from the supplier	5	6.9%
9. Cooperation with the trade	4	5.5%
10. Information to trade and sales force	3	4.1%
11. Profiling in relation to competitors	2	2.7%
12. Store shelf requirement	1	1.4%
13. Assortment compatability	1	1.4%

LEBENSMITTEL-ZEITUNG, a West German trade magazine, published, in

1975, the results of a survey of 310 supermarket chains with various organizational setups. Decision makers responsible for the buying and the selling functions of the companies were asked to state their opinion on the importance of 46 potentially relevant items of information related to the introduction of six specified new products. The results of the study were as follows (the 46 items of information were converted into 20 decision criteria): (Lebensmittel-Zeitung 1975, cited from Bauer 1980, pp. 207, 295-296 and 432. Our translation.)

		Cited as important (Percentage of respondents)
1.	Product's advantages and value for the consumer	47%
2.	Development of the market	40%
3.	Type and extent of the consumer advertising	38%
4.	Purchase and sales price; introductory price	35%
5.	Product (description)	35%
6.	Space-saving transportation and store package	34%
7.	Results of market and store tests	32%
8.	Gross margin	32%
9.	Market targent correctly identified	31%
10.	Sales and market share potential	29%
11.	Potential increase in profits and sales	29%
12.	Results of consumer interest survey	26%
13.	Supplementing the assortment	24%
14.	Product quality	22%
15.	Package or change in package	21%
16.	Display material	18%
17.	Sales assistance and sales promotion	17%
18.	Package size or weight	16%
19.	The manufacturer's production program	0%
20.	Turnover rate	0%

MONTGOMERY studied buying decision criteria in supermarket chains, using two alternative methods. These were multiple discriminant analysis and "gatekeeping" analysis. On the basis of interviews with buyers and attendance at buying committee meetings, he identified 18 potentially important decision criteria. He then conducted structured personal interviews with three buyers in different supermarket chains in the Boston area. The buyers were asked to evaluate a total of 124 new products according to the 18 criteria, and the buyers also told whether the products were accepted or rejected.

The list of decision criteria was as follows: (Montgomery 1975, pp. 256-257.)

- Promotion (sampling & couponing)
- Company reputation (manufacturer)
- Quality
- Newness

- Introductory allowances
- Competition
- Packaging
- Gross margin
- Advertising
- Private label (compete with ...)
- Guarantee (of movement)
- Distribution (nation/region/local)
- Broker
- Sales presentation
- Category volume
- Category growth potential
- Shelf space
- Cost (price)

The data set was first analysed with the help of multiple discriminant analysis. When nine variables were included in the model, 86 percent of the new product decisions were classified correctly. "The first six variables, in descending order of the absolute magnitude of their canonical coefficients, are private label, cost, category volume, packaging, competition, and newness." (Montgomery 1975, p. 259.)

Gatekeeping analysis results in a hierarchical threshold model, where the criteria are ordered like a tree diagram with the most important criteria on the top. Company (manufacturer) reputation turned out to be most decisive, followed by newness. Other important criteria were promotion, advertising, category volume, sales presentation and competition. Figure B-2 presents the entire model.

Inherent in gatekeeping analysis is a contingency concept; for example, depending on whether the product is considered to be significantly new or only slightly new, either advertising or category volume is the next criterion to be considered. There is, however, no attempt to explain these matters in Montgomery's article. Nor does he discuss why the two methods, applied to the same data set, give such different results.

JOHNSON presents the findings of a study of supermarket-chain buying behavior, conducted by Forecast Market Research Ltd. (Johnson 1976.) The researchers conducted lengthy personal, unstructured interviews with 20 directors and senior buyers of the major supermarket chains in the UK. From Johnson's presentation, we can identify the following decision criteria:

- The new product: the category it falls into and what it is going to do for the chain's position;
  * nutritional value
  * increase in convenience

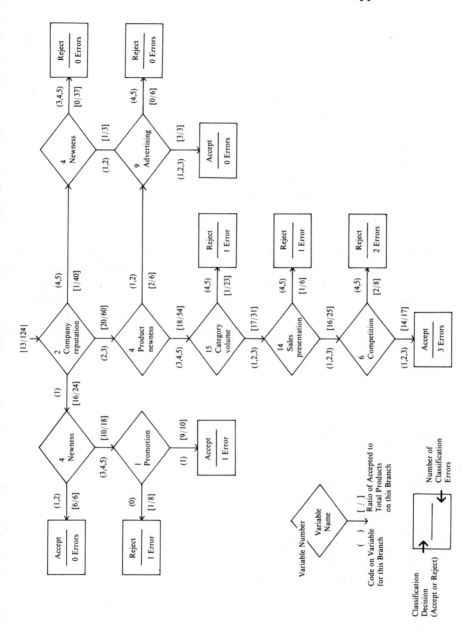

Figure B-2: Montgomery's Gatekeeping Analysis (Source: Montgomery 1975, p. 261.)

* improvement in economy
* a product development offering a tangible benefit, either to the housewife, or to the trader, or to both

- The support factors;
    * the manufacturer behind the launch
    * the manufacturer's track record
    * the manufacturer's relation with the Multiple
    * the new-product presentation
    * advertising support
    * the new product's price
    * the new product's packaging

- The deal; which the buyer can negotiate on behalf of his organization

LINDQVIST conducted a comprehensive study of the interrelations between food manufacturers and the four largest grocery chains in Finland. His method was unstructured interviews with various decision makers in retailing companies as well as with suppliers. From his text, we can extract the following decision criteria applied by the chains when selecting new products. (Lindqvist 1976, pp. 51, 54, 59, 74, 81, 87 and 88. Our translation.) The first five are claimed to be the most important:

- Product quality
- Product's demonstrated sales potential
- Supplier's price policy
- Supplier's marketing support
- Supplier's delivery reliability

- Supplier's market share
- Supplier's cooperativeness
- Supplier's overall reliability
- Product consumer value
- Product sales forecast
- Existence of distributor brands
- Product's origin (Finnish or foreign)
- Possibility for reciprocal purchases
- Buying conditions
- Product image
- Supplier's sales force
- Tactical considerations

PROGRESSIVE GROCER has published the findings from a study of grocery buyers' information needs, conducted by A. C. Nielsen. (Progressive Grocer 1978.) It is a follow-up on a study done ten years earlier, presented in Graf 1968 and Mueller & Graf 1968. The study was based on a mail survey among 99 headquarter buyers and observations from attendence at 137 new product presentations at buying sessions in 11 grocery distributor companies.

According to the survey, the buyers consider the following information topics to be very important for their new item decisions (averages of ratings on a scale to 100):

1. Consumer advertising (Television, print, spending, frequency)   89
2. Introductory terms (Ad & display allowances, discounts,
   how paid, buy-in-time)   86
3. Consumer promotion (Couponing, premiums, cents off, sampling, etc.)   81
4. Why item was developed (Consumer need,
   better product, line extention, etc.)   79
5. Description of item (Name, content, size, pack, cost margin data)   74
6. Consumer acceptance (Test market information, sales results)   71
7. Samples (Headquarter and store sampling)   60
8. Manufacturer recommendations (Initial order,
   distribution and merchandising information)   49

BAUER has published a very detailed survey of the literature covering the entire field of reseller assortment building. His study did not, however, include any empirical study of its own. The book comprises analyses in many subfields, such as assortment policy, decision processes, information collection and processing and buying organization. The longest chapter treats buying criteria. (Bauer 1980, pp. 225-313.) Here, Bauer begins by presenting an analytical-deductive survey of criteria, based on economic theory, management theory, organizational theory and other general social science theory constructs.

From this account one can extract a variety of criteria used in the reseller's evaluation of new products. The following is our attempt to summarize and structure Bauer's exposition: (Bauer 1980, pp. 227-281. Our translation of key terms.)

1. Characteristics of the decision situation
  - Evidence of consumer demand
    * Sales in other regions, store types, resellers, etc.
    * Sales trend of the product group

  - Indicators of acceptability and expected sales
    * Product characteristics, defining the salability, marketability or market adaptation of the product - especially an assessment of the product's consumer value, relative to that of current products
    * Test market sales results

   * The producer's marketing competence and the quality of the promotion measures that he uses or plans to use

- Assortment considerations
  * Possibilities of integrating the product into the current assortment in relation to type of stores, shelf space and competitive position
  * Whether the product fits into the current assortment
  * Whether the product contributes to making the assortment different from those of competitors
  * Whether the assortment can or should be expanded
  * Number of substitute products in the assortment, degree of substitution and gross margin of substitutes

- Revenue and cost effects, and risks
  * Prices
  * Conditions
  * Rate of turnover
  * Miscellaneous

- (Illegal) anticompetitive behavior
  * Excessive introductory allowances
  * Shelf and show window rentals
  * Advertising support
  * Taking over functions like price labeling and shelf care
  * Illegal discount offers
  * Corruption, bribery and preferential treatment

2. *Characteristics of the manufacturer and characteristics of the manufacturer-trade relation*

   2.1 *Manufacturer image*
      - General business behavior
        * Reliable and diligent order processing
        * Compliant treatment of complaints
        * Reliable and flexible deliveries
        * Meeting delivery schedules
        * Miscellaneous
      - Marketing skills
        * Market position
        * Market share
        * Success with previous new product introductions
        * Consumer awareness and attitudes

   2.2 *Conflict handling in the introduction of new products*
      - Degree of conflict or consonance between the manufacturer's goals and the distributor's goals
      - Manufacturer information on new products

      * Early information on new products and on product development
      * Objectivity and reliability in manufacturer information
   - Power balance between manufacturer and distributor

2.3 Partnership and cooperation between manufacturer and trade in the introduction of new products
   - Degree of cooperation
   - Domains of cooperation
   - Organization of cooperation

3. The manufacturer's sales efforts in the introduction of new products

3.1 Product and product mix
   - Product design
      * Consumer utility
      * Newness
   - Package design
      * Informative value
      * Ecological dimensions
      * Sales and consumer acceptance effects
      * Handling qualities (size, durability, etc.)
   - Varieties in the products line
      * Brand differentiation
      * Opportunites to reduce the risk of loss on excess stock
   - Manufacturer's product mix
      * Whether the manufacturer carries "full lines" in tastes and sizes.

3.2 Prices and terms
   - Prices
   - Discounts and allowances
   - Terms
   - Delivery conditions
   - Gross margin
   - Recommended consumer price
   - Payment conditions
   - Rate of turnover
   - Introduction price level

3.3 Communication
   - Trade-oriented communication
      * Adequacy of the message in terms of type and source of information
      * Adaptation to specific target groups
   - Consumer-oriented communication (advertising and sales promotion measures)
      * Volume of consumer advertising
      * Financial issues, i.e., whether cooperative advertising or not
      * Advertising argumentation
   - Point-of-purchase materials supplied by the manufacturer

3.4 Distribution channel policy and sales force organization
- The manufacturer's distribution channel policy
  * Whether the distributor will come to face stiff competition
  * Whether the distributor fits into the manufacturer's distribution strategy: product volumes, images, service levels, market segments, etc.
- Sales force organization
  * Qualifications and status of the salesmen
  * Organizational principles and structure

Bauer then continued to probe the literature on reseller assortment decision criteria. He selected 12 empirical studies, which include a total of 144 criteria. Based on the importance each criterion is said to have in the studies and on the number of studies mentioning each criterion, he compiled lists, where the criteria are ranked after importance. (See Figures 2-1 and 2-2 in Section 2.3, above.)

DOUGLAS examined decision criteria used by the British grocery trade when choosing between different brands of potato crisps (chips). (Douglas 1980. See also Douglas & McGoldrick 1981 and McGoldrick & Douglas 1983.) Based on a literature survey and pilot interviews in four distributor companies, he compiled a list of 19 decision criteria. He then conducted structured mail interviews with 73 buyers in various supermarket chains and cash-and-carry wholesalers. The respondents were asked to rate the various brands of potato crisps on each criterion, using a sevendigit scale from "no importance" to "primary importance."

The results show that there are certain differences between the chains and the cash-and-carry companies, but these differences are remarkably small. On the other hand, there are significant differences between criteria used for different brands of potato crisps. Douglas reported that, in most cases, the latter differences are due to various characteristics of the suppliers and their products. (Douglas 1980, pp. 212-228.)

The evaluations in the cash-and-carry companies resulted in the following ranking of the criteria: (Douglas 1980, p. 198 and Douglas & McGoldrick 1981, p. 20.)

1. Level of customer demand
2. Reliable delivery
3. General reliability
4. Quality of brand
5. Precise delivery
6. Above-the-line advertising
7. Size of promotional discounts
8. Size of annual growth discounts
9. Variety of crisp flavours
10. Size of quantity discounts

11. Competence of sales personnel
12. Accuracy of invoicing
13. Below-the-line advertising
14. Merchandising support
15. Length of credit
16. Range of snacks and nuts available
17. Variety of pack sizes available
18. Trade incentives
19. Other grocery lines available

NILSSON conducted a qualitative study of the assortment building function on the wholesale level of the two largest grocery chains in Sweden, one of them a union of consumer cooperatives and the other a retail cooperative. The study also included a fairly comprehensive literature survey, though most detailed within the subfield of assortment decision criteria. (Nilsson 1980, pp. 62-87. See also Nilsson 1976 and 1977.)

In his attempt to develop a generally valid list of criteria, Nilsson started with selecting ten empirical studies. He then tried to identify classes of criteria, so defined that all criteria mentioned in the studies (a total of 113), could be assigned to one and only one class. The resulting classification is identical with the one used in the present study, and reproduced in Section 2.3, above. Nilsson then went on to analyze the interrelations between the criteria, first on a logical-deductive basis, and then empirically. (See Figures 2-3 and 2-4, above.) He also made an attempt to assess the relative importance of the criteria, based on two considerations. Firstly, he supposed that the more often a criterion is mentioned in the ten empirical studies, the more important it is. Secondly, it was supposed that the higher up in a deductively constructed hierarchy (Figure 2-3) a criterion is found, the more important it is.

SAUER examined the purchasing policy of West German retailers in relation to their own retail cooperative. (Sauer 1982a and 1982b.) His aim was, firstly, to identify what decision criteria the retailers apply when selecting new products, and secondly, to find explanations of why these criteria are applied.

Based on a literature survey and informal discussions with retailers, Sauer constructed a list of 28 decision criteria. These criteria were formulated as statements in a questionnaire with five-level Likert scales, and the questionnaires were distributed to 700 retailers in two retail cooperatives. There were 221 responses. The results were as follows, where the criteria are arranged in descending order of importance: (Sauer 1982a, pp. 90-93. Our translation.)

average

1. I trade only with wholesalers who deliver on time and reliably.   4.475
2. My assortment is determined by consumer demand.   4.376
3. I carry goods which have a good image among the customers.   4.330
4. I select goods according to their high rate of turnover.   4.290
5. I prefer visits from well-known representatives rather than new ones.   4.186
6. I order articles with which I have had good experience as a consumer (have eaten, drunk or used myself).   4.036
7. I make sure that articles which the retail cooperative advertises are in my store in sufficient number.   3.986
8. When accepting new products, I prefer to be cautious, as we have already experienced too many failures.   3.959
9. I carry goods which I as a customer would prefer to buy.   3.814
10. I prefer to carry products which my competitors do not have in their assortments.   3.810
11. If possible, I order only goods which I can get from my retail cooperative.   3.724
12. When selecting the goods, I rely more on my own experience than on the assortment recommendations of the retail cooperative.   3.706
13. I choose products which are also advertised in other media than television.   3.679
14. I choose products, which can guarantee a high gross margin.   3.633
15. I prefer to have goods in my assortment which are frequently advertised on TV.   3.534
16. I prefer to buy goods on which - as I know from experience - the manufacturers/suppliers frequently give special prices   3.525
17. I choose articles I can get from the same supplier.   3.457
18. I try to buy goods I can offer to the customers at lowest possible prices.   3.389
19. I carry articles for which the manufacturers/suppliers often offer discounts in the form of gifts.   3.276
20. I choose products on which there are high (monetary) allowances.   3.163
21. I prefer to conduct buying negotiations with persons with whom I could also discuss private matters, rather than with those who only talk business.   3.118
22. When selecting the goods, I rely more on my own experience than on the assortment recommendation of the manufacturers.   3.090
23. I find manufacturer brands better than distributor brands.   3.090
24. I order goods for which the manufacturers/suppliers take over the shelf service (price marking, filling up goods, checking latest sale dates, etc.).   2.968
25. I think that the multitude of articles on the order lists of the retail cooperative should be more restricted.   2.774
26. When an item is deleted from the order list of the retail cooperative, I delete it also from my assortment.   2.724
27. I make sure that *at least half* of my assortment consists of low price articles.   2.367
28. I think that female representatives/salespersons are more pleasant negotiating partners than male representatives.   2.362

At the next stage, Sauer did a factor analysis in an attempt to identify a pattern in the responses given by the retailers. The factor analysis resulted in the formulation of four factors: (Sauer 1982a, pp. 107-114.)

Factor 1: The desire for profit, where criteria 13, 19 and 20 had the highest factor loadings.

Factor 2: The desire for source concentration, where criteria 26, 17 and 11 had the highest factor loadings.

Factor 3: The personal consumption preference, where criteria 9 and 6 had the highest factor loadings.

Factor 4: The desire for increase in turnover, where criteria 18 and 27 had the highest factor loadings.

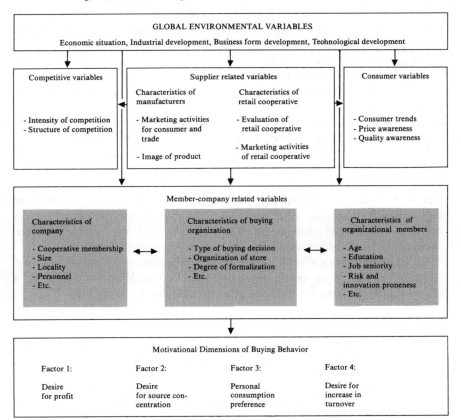

Figure B-3: Sauer's Frame of Reference for Buying Behavior in the Cooperative Retail Trade (Source: Sauer 1982a, p. 124. Our translation.)

Together, the four factors explain more than two thirds of the variance in the data set. Factor 1 is the most important, and it alone explains more than one third of the variance.

Sauer then proceeded to look for explanations of the four identified factors. He constructed a model, heavily influenced by the Webster & Wind industrial buying model. Sauer's model is presented in Figure B-3. In his empirical work, he tested a variety of relationships between the four motivational dimensions and various other variables, mainly belonging to the categories "member-company related variables" and "supplier related variables." The findings show several interesting correlations, though not sufficient to validate the entire model. Nevertheless, Sauer succeeded in showing that there are situational determinants for the decision criteria. Some of the results are:

- The tendency to use few supply sources (factor 2) is clearly related to what information sources the retailer is relying on.
- The tendency to use few supply sources (factor 2) depends on the retailer's attitudes toward the retail cooperative.
- Some consumer characteristics, such as price consciousness, influence the way in which the retailer tries to expand his sales (factor 4).
- If the retailer has a negative attitude toward the retail cooperative, he is more likely to rely on his personal experience (factor 3).
- The more often the retailer receives visits from the retail cooperative's representatives, the more important is the profit motive (factor 1) for him.
- Retailers for whom the profit criterion is important (factor 1) are more risk and innovation prone.

SWINNEN has examined the assortment decision process in Belgian supermarkets. (Swinnen 1982 and 1983.) He studied addition and deletion decisions separately, though he was well-aware of the interdependence between the two. Addition decision were, however, given most attention.

Based on interviews with 12 buyers in the four leading supermarket chains in Belgium, as well as on an extensive literature survey, Swinnen compiled "a reasonably exhaustive list of evaluation criteria:" (Swinnen 1983, pp. 83-85.)

I   Sales potential and customer acceptance
   - Test market results
   - Trade acceptance
   - Customer acceptance (marketing research, panel data)
   - Customer needs
   - Quality
   - Retail price (in relation to quality and the nearest substitute)
   - Degree of newness
   - Seasonality
   - Promotion program

- Advertising program
- Packaging (from the point of view of the customer)
- Volume potential of the product category
- Growth potential of the product category (product life cycle)
- Movement of similar products

II   *Profitability*
- Gross margin
- Rate of movement
- Conditions for payment
- Shelf space required
- Packaging (from the point of view of the supermarket)
- Manufacturers service (prepricing, in-store delivery, etc.)
- Freight charges (backhaul privilege)
- Commercial incentives
  - guarantee of stock return
  - introductory terms
  - special deals
  - discounts
  - other incentives (factory visits, etc.)

III   *Supplier evaluation*
- Size of the company
- Company reputation
  - market share
  - marketing program (advertising, promotion)
  - management
  - service (for instance through rack jobbing)
  - product policy (new product development)
  - price policy
  - production capacity
- Supplier reliability
- Delivery time
- Introductory program
  - timing of advertising and promotion
  - advertising and promotion allowances
  - special deals
  - advertising and promotion budget
- Trade discounts
- Distribution (nationally or regionally)
- Present supplier or not
- Domestic or foreign supplier
- Sales presentation by broker or supplier's representative)
- Presentation effectiveness
- Manufacturer's history (success with previous new product launches)

IV   *Concordance with assortment policy*
- Reflects objectives of the firm
- Quality and style
- Number of competing items
- Competition with private brands
- Similarity with existing items (product, packaging, size)
- Market concentration
- Number of suppliers for the product category
- Shelf space availability

As these criteria were operationalized, they were reduced to 15. Swinnen then used the conjoint analysis technique to identify the relative importance of each criterion. With data from seven buyers, the analyses resulted in the following ranking, expressing the average of the importance scores. (Swinnen 1983, p. 258.) Interestingly, Swinnen had one buyer distinguishing between national and distributor brands, with remarkable differences between these two product categories. (Swinnen 1983, p. 260.)

	Average of importance scores from seven buyers	*Importance of scores from one buyer*	
		Manufac-turer brands	*Distributor brands*
Quality	1	1	9
Performance of supplier	2	6	12
Results of test markets	3	13	8
Degree of newness	4	8	10
Growth potential of category	5	11	7
Gross margin	6	4	2
Cost of item	7	3	3
Composition of the product group	8	9	6
Packaging	9	10	13
Shelf space	10	2	1
Introductory allowances	11	5	4
Promotion program	12	7	5
Advertising program	13	12	11
Acceptance by competition	14	14	14
Term of payment	15	15	15

ANGELMAR and PRAS have conducted a study which differs from all other studies in several respects: the products studied are motion pictures; it deals with purchases by foreign distributor companies; data are collected through third-party sources. (Angelmar & Pras 1984.)

The study deals with U.S. distributors' acceptance of French motion pictures. Multiple discriminant analysis is used on a data set comprising ten predictor variables for 78 movies. The data stem mainly from facts published by movie magazines, expert ratings and short interviews with the producer, i.e., they do not presuppose collaboration with the buyers. Half of the movies were accepted by the importers. The most important factors appeared to be domestic sales figures, price, the occurrence of personal selling and the export system, implying direct sales as opposed to indirect. The percentage of correctly classified decisions was 95.

The ten explanatory variables were:

1. Product quality
2. Product adaptation
3. International character
4. Price
5. Export system
6. Personal selling
7. Domestic sales
8. Prior U.S. sales
9. U.S. awareness of director
10. U.S. awareness of actors

BIBLIOGRAPHY

Alderson, Wroe. *Dynamic Marketing Behavior. A Functionalist Theory of Marketing.* Homewood, IL: Irwin, 1965.

Amemiya, Takeshi. "Qualitative Response Models: A Survey," *Journal of Economic Literature* 19 (December 1981) 1483-1536.

American Marketing Association. *Marketing Definitions: A Glossary of Marketing Terms,* compiled by the Committee on Definitions of the AMA. Chicago, IL: AMA, 1960.

American Marketing Association. *Marketing Doctoral Dissertation Abstracts,* 1976, D.L. Shawver (ed.). Chicago, IL: AMA, 1977.

American Marketing Association. *Marketing Doctoral Dissertation Abstracts, 1977,* Edward W. Cundiff (ed.). Chicago, IL: AMA, 1978.

American Marketing Association. *Marketing Doctoral Dissertation Abstracts, 1978,* Edward W. Cundiff (ed.). Chicago, IL: AMA, 1979.

American Marketing Association. *Marketing Doctoral Dissertation Abstracts, 1979,* John K. Ryans, Jr. (ed.). Chicago, IL: AMA, 1980.

American Marketing Association. *Marketing Doctoral Dissertation Abstracts, 1980,* Thomas Greer (ed.). Chicago, IL: AMA, 1981.

American Marketing Association. *Marketing Doctoral Dissertation Abstracts, 1981,* Robert E. Witt (ed.). Chicago, IL: AMA, 1982.

Angelmar, Reinhard & Bernard Pras. "Product Acceptance by Middlemen in Export Channels," *Journal of Business Research* 12 (1984) 227-240.

Anthony, Robert N. *Planning and Control Systems. A Framework for Analysis.* Boston, MA: Harvard University, 1965.

Arora, Shiv Kumar. *"A Study of The Buyer-Seller Relationship, Buyer Influence, and New Product Selection Criteria in the Adoption of New Products by a Supermarket with a Buyer Merchandiser Committee."* Unpublished Ph.D. dissertation, Michigan State University, 1975.

Bauer, Hans H. *Die Entscheidung des Handels über die Aufnahme neuer Produkte. Eine verhaltenstheoretische Analyse* (Reseller Decisions on the Acceptance of New Products. A Behavior Theory Analysis). Berlin, F.R.G.: Duncker & Humblot, 1980.

Berens, John S. *"An Assortment Building Process Model of a Small, Independent Men's Wear Store."* Unpublished Ph.D. dissertation, Indiana University, 1969.

Berens, John S. "A Decision Matrix Approach to Supplier Selection," *Journal of Retailing* 47 (Winter 1971-1972) 47-53.

Borden, Neil H. Jr. *Acceptance of New Food Products by Supermarkets.* Boston, MA: Harvard University, 1968.

Brown, James R. & Prem C. Purwar. "A Cross-Channel Comparison of Retail

Supplier Selection Factors," in *Marketing in the 80's. Changes and Challenges.* Richard P. Bagozzi et al. (eds.). Chicago, IL: AMA, 1980, pp. 217-220.

Consumer And Industrial Buying Behavior. Arch G. Woodside, Jagdish N. Sheth & Peter D. Bennett (eds.). New York: North Holland, 1977.

Co-ops and Voluntaries. "How Buyers Foretell New Product Success," (December 1974) 30-32.

Davidson, William R., Alton F. Doody & Daniel J. Sweeney. *Retailing Management.* 4th edition. New York: Ronald Press Co., 1975.

Douglas, Robert A. *"Factors Influencing Multiple Grocery Retailers' and Cash & Carrys' Choice Between Suppliers of Major Brands of Potato Crisp."* Unpublished M.Sc. thesis, University of Manchester, Manchester, U.K., 1980.

Douglas, Robert A. & Peter J. McGoldrick. *"A Study of Supplier Selection by Multiple Retailers and Cash and Carries."* Occasional Paper No. 8109, Department of Management Sciences, University of Manchester Institute of Science and Technology, Manchester, U.K., 1981.

Doyle, Peter & Charles B. Weinberg. "Effective New Product Decisions for Supermarkets," *Operational Research Quarterly* 24 (1973) No. 1, 45-51.

Einstein, Samuel. "Merchandising the New Item," in *The Buyer's Manual* (revised edition). New York: The Merchandising Division, National Retail Merchants' Association, 1965.

Engel, James F. & Roger D. Blackwell. *Consumer Behavior,* 4th edition. Chicago, IL: The Dryden Press, 1982.

Engelman, Laszlo. "PLR 14.5 Stepwise Logistic Regression," in *BMDP Statistical Software,* W.J. Dixon (ed.). Los Angeles, CA: University of California Press, 1981.

The Food Trade Marketing Council. *The Selection and Introduction of New Items,* Report 5. Washington, DC: The Food Trade Marketing Council, 1964a.

The Food Trade Marketing Council. "How Food Distributors Buy Today," *Food Business* (December 1964b) 24 f.

Glaser, Barney G. & Anselm L. Strauss. *The Discovery of Grounded Theory. Strategies for Qualitative Research.* Chicago, IL: Aldine, 1967.

Gordon, Howard L. "How Important is the Chain Store Buying Committee?" *Journal of Marketing* (January 1961) 56-60.

Graf, Franklin H. "What Buyers Really Want from Salesmen", *Progressive Grocer* (September 1968) 66-70.

Grashof, John F. *"Information Managemant for Supermarket Chain Product Mix Decisions: A Simulation Experiment."* Unpublished Ph.D. dissertation, Michigan State University, 1968.

Grashof, John F. "Supermarket Chain Product Mix Decision Criteria: A Simulation Approach," *Journal of Marketing Research* (May 1970) 235-242.

Gripsrud, Geir & Leif Olsen. *Distribusjonssystem for dagligvarer: De fire gruppene på engrosleddet* (Distribution Systems for Convenience Goods: The Four Groups at the Wholesale Level). Oslo, Norway: Fondet for Markeds- og Distribusjonsforskning, 1975.

Gümbel, Rudolf. "Sortimentspolitik" (Assortment Policy), in *Handwörterbuch der Absatzwirtschaft*. Bruno Tietz (ed.). Stuttgart, F.R.G.: CE Poeschel Verlag, 1974, pp. 1884-1907.

Gümbel, Rudolf. "Sortiment und Sortimentspolitik" (Assortment and Assortment Policy), in *Handwörterbuch der Betriebswirtschaft. Vierte, völlig neu gestaltete Auflage,* Band I/3. E. Grochla & W. Wittman (eds.). Stuttgart, F.R.G.: CE Poeschel Verlag, 1976, pp. 3563-3573.

Heeler, Roger M., Michael J. Kearney & Bruce J. Mehaffey. "Modelling Supermarket Product Selection," *Journal of Marketing Research* (February 1973) 34-37.

Hileman, Donald G. & Leonard A. Rosenstein. "Deliberations of a Chain Grocery Buying Committee," *Journal of Marketing* (January 1961) 52-55.

Hill, Roy W. & Terry J. Hillier. *Organisational Buying Behavior. The Key to More Effective Selling to Industrial Markets*. London, U.K.: Macmillan, 1977.

Hix, John Lloyd. *"An Inquiry Into the Decision Criteria Used by Men's Wear Buyers in Department and Specialty Stores in Determining Whether to Include a New Product in Their Product Offering."* Unpublished Ph.D. dissertation, University of Arkansas, 1972.

Hutt, Michael D. *"The New Product Selection Process of Retail Buying Committees: An Analysis of Group Decision-Making."* Unpublished Ph.D. dissertation, Michigan State University, 1975.

Hutt, Michael D. "The Retail Buying Committee: A Look at Cohesiveness and Leadership," *Journal of Retailing* 55 (Winter 1979) 87-97.

Høst, Viggo & Jerker Nilsson. *"Choice Criteria for the Assortment Decisions of a Supermarket Chain."* Paper presented at the annual meeting of the European Marketing Academy in Grenoble, France, 1983.

Jick, Todd D. "Mixing Qualitative and Quantitative Methods: Triangulation in Action," *Administrative Science Quarterly* 24 (December 1979) 602-611.

Johnson, Maureen. *New Product Marketing and The Major Multiples*. London, U.K.: Forecast Market Research Ltd, 1976.

Johnston, Wesley J. "Industrial Buying Behavior: A State of the Art Review," in *Review of Marketing 1981,* Ben M. Enis & Kenneth J. Roering (eds.). Chicago, IL: American Marketing Association, 1981, pp. 75-88.

Kast, Fremont E. "Organizational and Individual Objectives," in *Contemporary Management. Issues and Viewpoints,* Joseph W. McGuire (ed.). Englewood Cliffs, NJ: Prentice-Hall, 1974, pp. 150-180.

Kast, Fremont E. & James E. Rosenzweig. "Introduction," in *Contingency Views of Organization and Management,* Fremont E. Kast & James E. Rosenzweig (eds.). Chicago, IL: Science Research Associates, 1973, pp. vii-xi.

Kast, Fremont E. & James E. Rosenzweig. *Organization and Management. A Systems Approach,* 2nd edition. Tokyo, Japan: McGraw-Hill Kogakusha, 1974.

Kihlstedt, Curt. *Sortiment inom detaljhandeln* (Assortments within the Retail

Trade). Stockholm, Sweden: FFI, The Stockholm School of Economics and Business Administration, 1961.

Kotler, Philip. *Marketing Management: Analysis, Planning and Control,* 5th edition. London, U.K.: Prentice-Hall International, 1984.

Lebensmittel-Zeitung. "Entscheidungsbildung im Lebensmittelhandel" (Decision Formation in the Grocery Trade). Frankfurt, F.R.G., 1970.

Lebensmittel-Zeitung. "Die anonyme Macht. Einkaufsgremien im Lebensmittelhandel" (The Anonymous Power. Buying Organizations in the Grocery Trade). Frankfurt, F.R.G., 1975.

Lindqvist, Lars-Johan. *"Marknadsföring till återförsäljare. En studie av några dagligvaruleverantörers marknadsföring genom distributörsblocken i Finland"* (Marketing for Resellers. A Study of Some Convenience Goods Suppliers' Marketing Through the Grocery Chains in Finland). Unpublished dissertation, The Swedish School of Economics and Business Administration, Helsinki, Finland, 1976.

Maddala, G. S. *Limited-dependent and Quantitative Variables in Econometrics.* Cambridge, U.K.: Cambridge University Press, 1983.

Mallen, Bruce. "A Theory of Retailer-Supplier Conflict, Control and Cooperation," in *Distribution Channels: Behavioral Dimensions,* Louis W. Stern (ed.). Boston, MA: Houghton Mifflin, 1969, pp. 176-187.

McGoldrick, Peter J. & Robert A. Douglas. "Factors Influencing the Choice of a Supplier by Grocery Distributors", *European Journal of Marketing* 17 (1983) No. 5, 13-27.

McNeill, Neil. *How Retail Buying Decisions Are Made.* New York: National Retail Merchants' Association, 1962.

Montgomery, David B. "New Product Distribution: An Analysis of Supermarket Buyer Decisions," *Journal of Marketing Research* 12 (August 1975) 255-264.

Morrison, Donald G. "On the Interpretation of Discriminant Analysis," *Journal of Marketing Research* 6 (May 1969) 156-163.

Mueller, Robert W. & Franklin H. Graf. *"New Items in the Food Industry, Their Problems and Opportunities."* Special report to the Annual Convention of the Supermarket Institute, Cleveland, OH, May 20, 1968.

Nigut, William. "Benchmarks for Product Success," *Food Business* 5 (October 1958) No. 10, 11-12.

Nigut, William. "A Second Look at Buying Committees," *Supermarketing* (April 1972) 57-60.

Nilsson, Jerker. *"Acceptance of New Food Products by Distributors."* Paper presented at the annual meeting of the European Academy for Advanced Research in Marketing in Fontainebleau, France, 1976.

Nilsson, Jerker. "Purchasing by Swedish Grocery Chains", *Industrial Marketing Management* 56 (1977) 317-328.

Nilsson, Jerker. *Sortimentsbyggande. En studie av den centrala inköpsverksamheten i ICA och KF* (with a summary in English) (Assortment Building. A Study of

Purchasing Procedures in Two Swedish Grocery Chains). Lund, Sweden: EFL/ Studentlitteratur, 1980.

Nilsson, Jerker. *Det konsumentkooperativa företaget* (The Consumer Co-operative). Stockholm, Sweden: Rabén & Sjögren, 1983.

Pindyck, R. S. and D. L. Rubinfeld. *Econometric Models and Economic Forecast,* 2nd edition. New York: McGraw-Hill, 1981.

Progressive Grocer. "New Item Study - Part II: The Buyer - Through the Needle's Eye at the Buying Office." (November 1978) 55-60.

Rhenman, Eric. *Organization Theory for Long-Range Planning.* Chichester, U.K.: Wiley, 1973.

Robinson, Patrick J., Charles W. Faris & Yoram Wind. *Industrial Buying And Creative Marketing.* Boston, MA: Allyn & Bacon, 1967.

Sauer, Klaus. *Das Einkaufsentscheidungsverhalten im genossenschaftlichen Lebensmitteleinzelhandel. Eine empirische Untersuchung* (Buying Behavior in the Cooperative Grocery Retail Trade. An Empirical Study). Göttingen, F.R.G.: Vandenhoeck & Ruprecht, 1982a.

Sauer, Klaus. "Das Einkaufs-Entscheidungsverhalten im genossenschaftlichen Lebensmitteleinzelhandel - eine empirische Untersuchung" (Buying Behavior in Cooperative Grocery Retail Trade - an Empirical Study). *Zeitschrift für das gesamte Genossenschaftswesen* 32 (1982b) 7-17.

Shipley, David D. "Resellers' Supplier Selection Criteria for Different Consumer Products," *European Journal of Marketing,* 19 (1985) No. 7, 26-36.

Simon, Herbert A. "On the Concept of Organizational Goals," in *Contingency Views of Organization and Management.* Fremont E. Kast & James E. Rosenzweig (eds.). Chicago, IL: Science Research Associates, 1973, pp. 120-137.

Stern, Louis W. & Adel I. El-Ansary. *Marketing Channels.* 2nd edition. Englewood Cliffs, NJ: Prentice-Hall, 1982.

Sweitzer, Robert W. *"The Behavioral Factors Affecting the Flow of Information in the Buyer-Seller Dyad."* Unpublished Ph.D. dissertation, Michigan State University, 1974.

Swinnen, Gilbert. *"Supermarket Chain Product Mix Decisions."* Paper presented at the annual meeting of the European Academy for Advanced Research in Marketing in Antwerp, Belgium, 1982.

Swinnen, Gilbert. *"Decisions on Product-Mix Changes in Supermarket Chains."* Unpublished Ph.D. dissertation, University of Antwerp, Belgium, 1983.

University Microfilms International. *Current Research on Marketing. A Catalogue of Doctoral Dissertations, 1977-1982.* London, U.K.: UMI, 1982.

Webster, Frederick E. Jr. & Yoram Wind. *Organizational Buying Behavior.* Englewood Cliffs, NJ: Prentice-Hall, 1972.

Wind, Jerry. "Toward a Change in the Focus of Marketing Analysis: From a Single Brand to an Assortment," *Journal of Marketing* 41 (October 1977) 12 & 143.

FIGURES

Author index

Subject index